MAKING HUMAN RIGHTS REAL

MAKING HUMAN RIGHTS REAL

Filip Spagnoli

Algora Publishing
New York

ISBN-13: 978-0-87586-569-0 (trade paper)
ISBN-13: 978-0-87586-570-6 (hard cover)
ISBN-13: 978-0-87586-571-3 (ebook)

Library of Congress Cataloging-in-Publication Data —

Spagnoli, Filip.
  Real human rights / Filip Spagnoli.
      p. cm.
  Includes bibliographical references and index.
    ISBN 978-0-87586-569-0 (soft cover: alk. paper) — ISBN 978-0-87586-570-6 (hard
cover: alk. paper) — ISBN 978-0-87586-571-3 (ebook) 1. Human rights. I. Title.

  JC571.S7383 2007
  323—dc22
                              2006037954

Parts of this book were published previously by Cambridge Scholars Press and are
reprinted with their kind permission.

Front Cover: Woman Holding a Burning Book, Photographer: Sven Hagolani
© Sven Hagolani/zefa/Corbis

Printed in the United States

To Iwona

TABLE OF CONTENTS

PREFACE

Most books on the theory of human rights are written by and for scholars and are not easily accessible to other people. However, scholars are clearly not the most vulnerable part of humanity and may therefore find their theoretical insights not very useful. Those who would find these insights useful, namely victims (or possible victims) of human rights violations and grassroots activists trying to protect these victims, are often not attracted to scholarly works.

Now one may ask: how would those people benefit from a clear understanding of the theory of human rights? Would they not be better served by some practical, strategic and organizational guidance, financial assistance, etc.? The answer is that they need both, because even when a brutal leader seems to be violating people's rights without explanation and without any compunction, if pressed he will offer some kind of justification for his actions. For example, he may try to explain that rights are not universal. Or that some rights may be sacrificed for the sake of other rights, or for some other "greater good". A theoretical argumentation about universality and interdependence of rights may come in handy when questioning these justifications and opposing these violators.

Such a theoretical background to the system of human rights is what this book tries to offer. It profits from scholarly achievements and translates these into ordinary and accessible language aimed at a general public. But it goes further. In addition to a theoretical description of the most important characteristics of the system of human rights, it also offers a practical discussion of the means to make these rights real, to turn them from words into facts, from moral claims into everyday reality. After all, it is obvious that theoretical attacks on justifications of rights violations will never be enough.

The book is easily accessible to those of us who are not yet familiar with the intricacies of the system of human rights. This is not a highly specialized philosophical or legal treatise but a first, general introduction aimed at those who are promoting human rights, either because their own rights are violated or because they are in a position to help victims or to construct institutions that can protect rights and make them real. It can easily find its place between on the one hand the more specialized works and on the other hand the usual general public works on human rights that too often focus on specific instances of rights abuses at the expense of a more general approach focused on the logic in the system of human rights.

An inevitable result of this approach is a certain lack of depth. It is difficult to be at the same time wide-ranging, complete, accessible and profound, especially in a relatively small number of pages. Those who feel the need to go somewhat deeper after reading this book may find some interesting references to other books at the end.

One obvious characteristic of this book is its combination of lightness of tone and seriousness of purpose. Nuances, jargon and detailed philosophical, legal and political discussions are avoided as much as possible. The purpose is serious because I wanted to transmit certain messages about human rights to people who perhaps have not yet reflected deeply on the subject but whose rights may be routinely violated. In doing so, I wanted to offer these people a tool to protect themselves.

In the course of my narrative, there are many occasions where I mention attitudes, institutions and other mechanisms that are required to make rights real. As I have chosen not to repeat myself in a summary, it was only fair to offer the reader a tool to make his or her own summary. Therefore, every time I mention the reality of rights, words like reality, real, realization, etc. are put in italics.

Introduction: Truth and Politics

First, let's consider the status of the narrative contained in this book and more in general the relationship between truth and politics. The thoughts on human rights and democracy that I will present here are mere proposals and attempts. I do not pretend to proclaim the truth about rights and democracy. If there is any truth in the world at all, it is probably not in the domain of politics, morality and values. It is likely that all we can say about such subjects is mere opinion. However, even if we cannot prove anything or be certain about anything in politics, this does not mean that all opinions are equally valid. There can be good and bad opinions because opinions are based on arguments and reasons, and arguments and reasons can be strong or weak or completely lacking. If all opinions were of the same quality then no one would ever try to convince anyone of anything.

Opinions are, by nature, non-despotic: they cannot be forced on you. The truth can. No one can escape the truth. The laws of physics for example have a despotic character. You have to accept them. Opinions can be accepted or rejected, depending on the force of the arguments for or against, on your personal disposition, your intellectual powers of understanding, etc. Another characteristic of opinions is that they are part of a contradictory world of different opinions. An opinion exists only as long as its contrary also exists. If the latter ceases to exist, then the former becomes what we may call some form of truth, at least to the extent that we may give this label to an opinion that is the object of a worldwide consensus.

Truth implies consensus. Who dares to resist the truth? Only a fool or a moron. Truth eliminates debate because no one contradicts the truth. As long as someone who is neither a fool nor a moron contradicts the truth and gives good reasons for doing so, we have not yet attained the level of truth and remain in the world of opinion. This world is one of plurality and contradiction; the world of truth is one of uniformity. Only when everyone is convinced and no good reasons or arguments against are left can we claim to have identified something like the truth. Even when some opinions are predominant, they remain mere opinions as long as good counter arguments are available, or, in other words, as long as contradictory opinions based on good arguments — and not mere prejudices — are available.

Like everyone who expresses an opinion, I also would like to see my opinions, expressed in this book, elevated to the status of truth. But that depends on many things: the force of my arguments, the disposition of my readers, etc. It is not a result that I can determine or even predict. If I would force this elevation — on the condition that I would have the power to do so — then I would not be acting democratically and I would therefore be incoherent. Democratic politics does not take place in the world of truth or the world of uniformity and despotism. Opinions are the fabric of democracy. Democracy is the game of different and contradictory opinions, some of which become temporarily predominant because they are backed by the better arguments or the arguments that can convince a majority, on the condition that we speak about a perfect democracy unhindered by manipulation. The predominant opinions then inform government policy, but non-predominant ones continue to exist and continue to make their case in an effort to become predominant themselves. If these other opinions no longer exist, then it is not opinion but what has become accepted as truth that informs government policy. This can and does happen, even in the case of perfectly democratic governments. But it is not typical of a democracy and is not its essence. One can even say that the job of a democracy is finished when it happens.

For example, that it is good policy to control inflation is no longer an opinion. There are no longer good arguments for the opposite policy and everyone is convinced that it is a good policy. Hence, there is no democratic debate for or against the fight against inflation. The policies of all governments, including democracies, are inspired by this truth, but this has nothing to do with democracy. Democracy can only enter the stage when different actors present different and contradictory opinions, for example opinions regarding abortion. There is intense debate about this subject. The predominance and hence also government policy shifts from one side to the other.

But what we see in the example of abortion and in many other controversies is that democracy does not only stop when an opinion is elevated to the level of truth. It also stops when contradictory opinions continue to exist but are no longer argued. Proponents and opponents of abortion have practically stopped giving reasons and arguments. They just throw citations from the Bible or general and vague claims of rights at one another. In fact, their opinions have not been elevated to the level of truth but have rather descended to the level of prejudices or "feelings" or beliefs. Democracy requires opinions, nothing more and nothing less. Opinions are based on arguments and reasons, not on evidence, proof, certainty, prejudices, feelings or beliefs. Democracy only has a function when there can be debate and there can only be debate when there are opinions, not when there is more or less, not when everything is either truth or belief. Of course, beliefs should not be excluded from democratic politics, just as truth should not be excluded. Beliefs can be a powerful force behind debates. They can inspire thinking and discussion, but they will never be the essence of democracy. If there is nothing more than beliefs, then there is no democracy.

So truth can enter democracy — democratic governments would be literally stupid not to allow this — but it will never be its essence. When truth becomes the essence of politics, democracy dies. This can happen when people forget that what they believe is an opinion rather than the truth. They are unable or unwilling to see that other, contradictory opinions based on good arguments continue to exist, and try to transform politics from a space of discussion into a machine for the application of the truth, of their truth. Other opinions are suppressed because they are not recognized as valid opinions based on arguments. Instead, they are, quite logically, deemed to be mistakes or errors, or even lies, because they contradict the beliefs of those who believe to possess the truth. And who would not admit action against errors or lies?

This unwarranted renaming of opinions into truths, and the subsequent actions against opinions that are not in fact errors or lies but are real opinions based on sound arguments, destroys debate and democracy. Politics becomes a tool to transform reality, to shape the world according to some theory or utopia considered to be the true teaching. This is the mindset we find in Fascism or adherents of other ideologies who are convinced that they possess the truth and are unable or unwilling to recognize the views of others as valid opinions based on sound arguments. Everything outside of their worldview is "false" and "needs to be corrected" (take also the infamous re-education camps of communism) or even destroyed if correction is not possible. Politics takes on the characteristics of truth: uniformity and despotism.

If you see yourself as the bearer of truth rather than one who holds a particularly well-argued opinion, then you feel that you have to suppress other views. You are morally obliged to act against mistakes and lies. Allowing someone to lie or to live a life of mistakes is immoral. Such a person is not someone who happens to hold another opinion based on arguments that, according to you, are less successful, and whose opinions have to be respected. Rather, he or she must be stupid or even of bad faith, and must be re-educated in order to access the truth. Democratic argumentation and discussion will not help in these cases because argumentation requires a target that is sensitive to good arguments and hence not stupid, and is of good faith. And in any case, truth does not need arguments. It is self evident and, if not, merely requires explanation. But explanation does not help either when the target is stupid or of bad faith. Force is then the only means left. This is the fatal logic that drives people who believe themselves to be the holders of truth away from democracy and into tyranny.

A writer or philosopher is often one of those persons who believe themselves to be holding the truth. He or she is therefore also tempted into this logic and may want to determine social life and shape it in the form of his or her theories. Democratic politics and the struggle between contradictory opinions are then replaced by a uniform world reflecting a theory that pretends to be the truth rather than one opinion among many. Political life is determined by one of its actors and is no longer the struggle between actors. Even a philosopher of democracy can be tempted by this logic. No matter how democratic his or her philosophy, it will become corrupted when it is seen as the truth rather than one opinion among others. This philosophy has to be imposed when it is seen as the truth, because one cannot accept mistakes or lies. Only if it is seen as one opinion among others, even an opinion based on amazingly good arguments, and only if it is introduced into democratic debate rather than imposed as the truth, can it remain internally coherent. The democratic philosopher has to propose instead of impose, and then has to see what happens with the theory in the public debate. If the arguments are really sound, then people may accept them and the theory can become the accepted truth. If not, the philosopher has to try again. Truth in politics can be recognized as a result of debate but the debate should never be skipped, and the truth can never emerge as a result of individual efforts.

If people believe that they hold the truth and are unable to recognize that other people's beliefs may (also) be based on sound arguments, then they enter into a dangerous logic of mistakes, lies, suppression, imposition, and re-education. However, this does not mean that democratic politics cannot or should not be based on strong beliefs. Participants must believe that their opinions are valid and that they have good reasons for believing in these opinions, and they can act according to these opinions. Democratic action can be inspired by theory — and even should be, if it wants to be intelligent and something more than pure activism. But it should never forget that others may be inspired differently and have sound reasons to follow other opinions. Action inspired by theory has to take place within the democratic game of competing opinions and should not replace this game by the effort to impose something that is mistaken for the truth and that is in fact merely one opinion in a setting of many competing opinions.

Political theory can inspire political action. Democracy is therefore more than pure activism. But theory is also formed by democratic political action. The meaning of concepts like democracy, justice, liberty, etc. is framed by political debate and discussion, and not solely by the individual thinking of philosophers. But this framing is provisional because debates never end and new arguments in favor of some opinion can always emerge or old arguments can acquire more power.

So, no matter how vigilant we should be about the separation of truth and politics, we should not exaggerate and completely separate theory and action. On the one hand, if we introduce truth into politics, then we run the risk of entering into a logic of mistakes, lies and suppression and we replace the political struggle between opinions by a world in which action is completely determined by some theory about what is true and what is not. Action becomes completely subordinated to theory. On the other hand, theory should be allowed to inspire action because otherwise action is dumb. But this inspiration should be one among many contradictory kinds of inspiration, and should be conscious of the fact that it is an opinion rather than the truth, no matter how good the reasons are in favor of this opinion.

Theory should be allowed to inspire action, but it should also be allowed to result from action. Democratic political participation and discussion generate theory and are not simply the application of a theory already given before the action starts. Moreover, the theory generated by politics has some advantages compared to individually generated theories. Democratic discussion allows the appearance of different arguments, which improves the quality of thinking. Many brains put together are smarter than one. Theory is not in some way "higher" than or superior to action, because it results from action. Neither is action more important than words, because no wise action without wise words. Clear thinking makes actions more efficient, makes it easier to convince opponents, etc. Those who think can assist those who act, although they should never determine actions completely and forget how much they depend on action.

So, in a way, politics does not start but ends with theory.

> [P]olitics is not the application of Truth to the problem of human relations but the application of human relations to the problem of truth. . . . Truth in politics seems, as William James said of truth in general, to be something which is "made in the course of experience" rather than something discovered or disclosed and then acted upon. . . . [T]ruth [is] . . . a product of certain modes of common living rather than the foundation of common life.[1]

Except then for those "truths" that are the foundation of common life and deliberation, namely human rights. These rights are in a sense not the product of common life but its beginning. This does not mean that they are beyond debate or that they do not have to compete in the market place of ideas. They are indeed actively contested and people have to make the case for them. However, one cannot fail to notice the inconsistency of those rejecting human rights: their rejection takes place in the public space created by human rights. It is difficult to reject human rights without using them.

This meta-status of human rights, or the recognition of the way in which they create common life and political deliberation rather than resulting from

---

1 Barber, B.R. 1984, *Strong Democracy, Participatory Politics for a New Age*, Berkeley/Los Angeles: University of California Press, p. 64-5.

it, is apparent from the fact that they are not protected by normal laws but by national constitutions. The people in a democracy, via their legislators, cannot easily repeal the laws protecting human rights. These laws precede and guarantee politics and are therefore independent of politics; they are untouchable. Popular sovereignty is limited. Politics is insulated against the absolute, but at the same time it is protected by another kind of absolute. The principles that make democratic politics possible acquire a kind of absolute value, without ascending to the realm of truth because human rights are contested, even though it seems logically difficult to contest the institutions necessary for the protection of contestability. That would amount to contesting contestability.

Too much relativism is just as dangerous for politics as too much certainty. If there is too much certainty, then debate and plurality disappear, but if there is too little certainty — e.g. no certainty as to the value of the right of free speech — then debate will also disappear because the institutions that protect it will disappear. Either we will be destroyed by fanatics with their own certainty because we will lack the conviction to defend ourselves and our values, or we will lose interest in our values. People who are only interested in their own subjective opinions and desires and who disregard intersubjectivity are just as dangerous to democracy and human rights as people who force their so-called objective opinions on others.

CHAPTER 1. UNIVERSAL RIGHTS

CULTURAL RELATIVISM

Most people know their human rights pretty well.[1] What is less obvious is that they fully understand the meaning of their rights, the links between them and the extent of their application. I will discuss these matters first because they have an impact on the ways in which we can turn rights into facts.

What is the meaning and significance of human rights? Let us start with universality. Proponents of human rights, and I am obviously one of them, believe that human rights have a universal meaning and significance. Whether they believe this to be the truth or just their opinion, they strongly argue that human rights are the equal property of all human beings. Nobody has more or less rights than anybody else. No groups, nations, classes or races should be excluded from the protection of human rights.

This normative characteristic is of course inherent in the expression it-self — human rights are rights of all humans — but it is not universally ac-cepted. Many people, in particular those who benefit from violations of other people's rights, reject the claim that human rights are universal, primarily because non-universality would allow the continuation of rights violations

---

1 Nevertheless, for the sake of clarity and in order to express what exactly I personally have in mind when writing about rights, I have added an appendix listing the main human rights as they can be found in the basic international documents (declarations and treaties).

and hence the continuation of the benefits that almost inevitably result from violations. Somebody always benefits from the harm inflicted on others; otherwise there would be no harm inflicted.

However, these benefits are rarely given in justification of non-universality because a justification is usually a moral undertaking, and therefore cannot start from the premise that benefits for someone justify harm inflicted on someone else. A more common justification for the claim that human rights do not apply universally can be found in the theory of cultural relativism or in some variation of it. The point of this chapter is to show that this is not a valid justification — it is at most an excuse — and that there is therefore a *prima facie* reason to accept the universality of human rights.

Cultural relativism is essentially a moral theory, even when it is used for an immoral purpose. It rejects the worldwide application of human rights because it rejects the imposition of the culture and norms of the West on other cultures. Universal human rights are said to imply the immoral destruction of other cultures, which in turn diminishes the well-being of the people of those cultures. Identity, especially cultural identity, and a feeling of belonging, are important for everyone's well-being. This is the moral basis of cultural relativism.

The underlying hypothesis of this theory is that human rights are part of the culture of the West, typical of this culture, and compatible only with this culture. They are therefore Western rights rather than universal norms. Under this hypothesis, the worldwide promotion of what we call *human* rights can be seen as the imposition of the culture of the West. Human rights in this view belong to the cultural identity of the West with its emphasis on individualism and individual freedom. Other cultures have other identities, values and norms. They may cherish harmony and collective goals more than individualism, discipline more than freedom, respect for authority more than democracy, tranquility more than adversarial politics, the afterlife more than free consumption and maximum gratification in the present life, etc. Hence, they will have norms that are different from the norms of the West and different from the application of human rights for every individual. Their norms may even be opposed to human rights.

Respect for the cultural identity and the well-being of other people means that they should be allowed to adhere to these norms and to violate human rights when these rights come into conflict with their own norms.

Insistence on human rights, then, could mean disrespect, erosion of cultural identity, and hence also erosion of individual well-being.

According to cultural relativism and its many overt and covert adherents, human rights have a claim to existence in the West, where they are part of the culture and are in accordance with cultural norms and values (such as individualism, conflict, etc.), but not in parts of the world where they are at best inappropriate and at worst damaging to cultural identities and therefore also to people who depend on culture for their personal identity and feeling of belonging.

Cultural relativism and its variations have filtered through into contemporary politics but they are not new. They have their origin in the struggle against colonialism. The West has indeed taken an offensive and even aggressive attitude towards other cultures. It asserted that it was an example for the rest, more developed, and better in all aspects. The territorial occupation of other countries or regions and their inclusion into the "Western Empire" was more easily achieved when the elites of those territories were co-opted, taught to admire and identify with the Western culture. But also the rest of the population of the "underdeveloped" or "backward" cultures was obliged to accept the Western values, norms, religion and practices, "for their own good". The interests of imperialism and colonialism were thus fostered under a pseudo moral guise, although some colonialists were undoubtedly sincere in their belief that imperialism served the universalization of morality rather than the other way around. In any case, whether sincere or not, the declared purpose was to improve other cultures by making them more like the West, to introduce progress and to eliminate "barbarism". However, the introduction of the culture of the West resulted in catastrophes. People were alienated from their cultures and uprooted, and a wonderful world of diversity was destroyed.

It seems difficult and unnecessary to argue against this. The crimes of the West are uncontested, even in the West. The problems start when colonialism and imperialism are linked to the promotion of human rights as an effort based on the belief in the universality of human rights. The opponents of rights universality argue that colonialism and imperialism were but one expression of Western universalism and Western contempt for other cultures, and that human rights policy is another, more modern expression of the same contempt. This policy is supposed to be a new and covert kind of colonialism and imperialism, so-called neo-colonialism, an intellectual and moral kind of colonialism that, just like old-style colonialism, wants to impose Western values, now without territorial occupation but still with commercial interests and moral superiority in the background.

The differences between old and new colonialism are said to be minimal, because the consequences for cultures are roughly the same. Cultures were destroyed during the era of real colonialism, and are again destroyed by the neo-colonialism of human rights promotion. Imposing the Western culture of rights outside of the West means that other cultures are forced to give up their own norms, values and practices, especially when these contradict human rights.

The promotion of human rights, in cases where it undermines a society's hierarchy and traditions, can alienate people from their culture and make them lose their sense of identity and belonging, and so causes some of the same problems as the ones caused by colonialism. People have to abandon their traditional way of life and have to start living according to the norms of the West, which means that ultimately they will start living an individualistic, egocentric and consumption-focused life, even where the resources are not suited to support such a life. If they do not live, think and act like Westerners and do not respect the norms of a Westerner, then they are seen as inferior, primitive, barbaric, uncivilized, irrational, prejudiced and in need of some Western enlightenment.

Many believe that Western supremacy is still a fact, although nowadays perhaps less a political and territorial fact than a cultural one. There is no longer integration into a larger territorial entity, but there still is integration into another cultural entity. Conquest and territorial expansion may be proceeding in a slightly subtler fashion, but economic assimilation, cultural imperialism and cultural expansion are alive and kicking. The West is still imposing its values and culture and is still disrespecting other cultures. Cultures and people still suffer, albeit perhaps less than a hundred years ago, because cultural expansion is much more difficult without territorial expansion. But the suffering is still important enough to be worried and to resist human rights policy. An effort to relieve suffering — which is basically what human rights policy is all about — is thereby depicted as the cause of suffering. It is no coincidence that many of the early adherents of cultural relativism were trained in Marxist dialectics.

I can agree that the loss of cultural identity or of a feeling of belonging causes suffering. But is there really a perfect analogy between colonialism and human rights policy, and does the acceptance of human rights necessarily mean the loss of identity and belonging? It is true that respect for human rights must lead to the abandonment of some cultural practices (although in most cases it must lead to the abandonment of distinctly non-cultural practices), but certainly not of all cultural practices and probably not the most important ones. Culture or identity is above all something that is in the mind. What is in the mind cannot cause harm and should never be abandoned. To the extent that culture is part of the mind, it enjoys complete protection by human rights. The global extension of human rights will never harm culture in this sense. The freedom of thought is perhaps the most fundamental human right and is an example of the way in which rights protect rather than harm culture (I will come back to this in a moment).

Human rights therefore do not require the loss of an entire culture or identity. But, of course, culture can only be embedded in the mind when there are practices that embed it, and these practices, contrary to an identity, can cause harm and rights violations. However, is change such a bad thing? The West has had to abandon or reform some of the elements of its culture (or cultures) in order to achieve a higher level of respect for human rights, and so have many other cultures. This has happened even without the prodding of human rights universalists. Cultural practices change anyway, so why not change them in the direction of human rights and why not try to encourage change in this direction rather than another?

Respect for human rights demands change now and again, but in doing so it does not make extraordinary demands on cultures. It merely wants to determine the direction of change, where change is inevitable in any case. And the change that it seeks to foster and direct never implies the abandonment of a given culture altogether. Human rights policy therefore is not in itself the cause of alienation, assimilation, cultural imperialism and the loss of identity and belonging.

Moreover, the link between culture on the one hand and practices that have to be abandoned in the name of human rights on the other hand, is often tenuous if not completely imaginary. The Koran for example does not impose female circumcision, and "disappearing" people is certainly not a common cultural practice in Latin America. The latter is never claimed to be the case, but the former is; and it seems that many violators simply try to use culture as a shield to protect their actions. They try to argue that there is somehow a link between their actions and culture, no matter how improbable that may be. They know that the theory of cultural relativism or some of its variations are so commonly accepted that they may be successful in using it as a justification of their actions. However, contrary to the spirit of cultural relativism, they do not have the interests of culture in mind, but use culture to protect their own interests and the benefits they reap from human rights violations.

The claim that the exercise of human rights threatens cultures becomes even more improbable once we understand that in many cases cultural practices do not have to give way to, but actually benefit from, human rights. Many human rights, and not just freedom of thought, provide mechanisms for the protection of identity and belonging, e.g., rights that protect tolerance, religious liberty, freedom of association, non-discrimination, etc. So the demand made by cultural relativism and its explicit or implicit followers, that there should be no hierarchy — political or moral — between cultures but instead equality and respect for diversity sounds like music in the ears of the proponents of human rights. It is no exaggeration to say that equality, respect and acceptance of diversity are the essence of human rights. Human rights are equal rights which create and protect a world of difference and tolerance.

Respect for cultural diversity should indeed be the rule. Human rights proponents would betray their philosophy in any other case — the only exception to the rule being those practices that violate human rights. There can be no respect for that, for many reasons but mainly because violations of human rights would make the defense of culture, diversity and equality in general much more difficult, even though in particular cases violations of rights may seem to be required by culture. Cultural relativists and others who want to protect culture should therefore embrace rather than dismiss human rights.

There are many things wrong with the claim that we should respect practices that violate human rights simply because these practices are said to be the expression of an authentic and equally respectable culture. Or with the similar claim that we should not reject these practices simply because they offend our sense of justice; our sense of justice being nothing more than that, namely *our* sense of justice, and other people may have another sense of justice, a sense based on their culture and just as valuable as our sense of justice.

First, most practices that violate rights are not expressions of culture but simply pretend to be (often, they do not even bother to pretend). And even when these practices are expressions of a culture, the requirement that they be abandoned is an attack on a small part of a culture, not on an entire culture. A culture is much more than some practices or some rights violations. Moreover, the extension of human rights is never an "attack"; it is simply a proposal for change. Cultures change and develop even without human rights policy. It is just a matter of steering this development in the proper direction.

Secondly, proponents of these claims adhere to a kind of amorality or positivism that they would not be willing to accept within their own culture. They (or we, for that matter) do not say that a criminal within their culture should be allowed to do what he does simply because he has a different "sense of justice" or because what he does is an expression of his "equally valuable and respectable" sub-culture. Not everything is acceptable in the name of culture.

Another claim, that the acceptance of human rights means the introduction of the culture of the West, can only be true if human rights are part of the essence of Western culture and are totally alien to other cultures. But this is obviously not the case. All cultures have values and principles that reflect the values embedded in human rights. And the West probably suffers just as many rights violations as any other culture. It has, for some centuries now, been struggling against certain of its own cultural practices that, from a rights point of view, are or were unacceptable.

This shows that demands for the modification of certain cultural practices are often based on other parts of the same culture which are more or less explicit expressions of a belief in human rights. So demands for change are not necessarily external to the culture in question. It is often an internal contradiction within a culture that one tries to resolve. So imperialism is not even a topic.

If human rights policy does not imply the introduction of the culture of the West, then it cannot be criticized for being an expression of a belief in cultural supremacy and cultural universality, at least not in principle. Some Westerners may believe that human rights promotion is part of the promotion of Western culture, the development of the underdeveloped, and the re-placement of barbaric cultures with a superior one. But they are wrong. Only individual violators or certain kinds of practices may be barbaric, inferior or underdeveloped, and these violators and practices can be found everywhere, in every culture. A culture as such is never inferior and the equality between cultures is something which human rights promoters must and do accept, in the first place because both rights violations and humanitarian principles can be found in more or less equal measure in all cultures, and secondly be-cause rights require equal tolerance and respect for diversity.

An attitude of cultural superiority is incompatible with human rights pro-motion because human rights require tolerance, respect and equal rights, but also because cultural superiority entails an expulsion from humanity similar to the expulsion practiced by rights violators. The ideology of cultural su-premacy implies the inferiority of the other. The other is "less human", or not even human at all. This was a popular belief at the time of colonialism. The same notion of expulsion from humanity lies behind many rights violations because these violations can only be justified when "the other" is labeled as something less than human. Rights promoters cannot (and do not have to) use the ideology of cultural supremacy because then they would betray ev-erything that rights stand for (tolerance, diversity, etc.) and they would ally themselves to the very people they fight, namely rights violators, colonialists, racists, and others who believe in the supremacy of one race above others.

There is no reason to link rights promotion to supremacy and racism. In fact, it is easy to return the compliment. Reserving rights to the West can be seen as a form of racism. People from other cultures also want respect for their rights. They are not docile victims full of cultural respect for their oppressing authorities. We should not accept that governments turn crimes into norms just because they happen to say that these crimes are an expres-sion of culture.

... OR CULTURAL ABSOLUTISM?

Respect for diversity cannot be an absolute principle. Diversity, identity and belonging are important to people, and cultural supremacy, ethnocen-trism, cultural disdain, assimilation, etc. are therefore unacceptable (and also unnecessary and even counterproductive for rights promotion). But rights are also important to people, and when rights and culture go opposite ways, then I think most victims of culture would ask us to give priority to their rights rather than to some aspect of their culture or identity. And it is they who should decide on this priority. Who else could? Certainly not some self-declared defender of culture who most likely has his own un-cultural reasons for defending rights violations, for example, the reason that he is also the violator.

One should never forget that cultures, diversity, identity and belonging are there for people, and that people are not there for cultures. Accepting violations for the sake of a culture means that this culture is more important than the people that are part of it. It means that people are an instrument for the continuation of culture and can be used or abused if this is required for their culture. This is something few people would accept. Even those who do not stop to defend the interests of culture do so because they believe that culture is important to people, not the other way around. And when culture becomes harmful to people, then respect for it should cease.

People must be treated as individuals, individuals for whom life in a group, identification with others and respect for a cultural heritage are important. They should not be treated as part of a culture that is sacred and inviolable and that has a right to harm individual members if necessary. A person has rights; a society or culture only has rights added to and in function of the rights of real people. Again, it is tempting to see this as an expression of Western individualism but essentially it is based on a global consensus. Groups are important to people and therefore deserve respect, but only to a certain extent. The limit is given by human rights. If a culture transgresses this limit, then this culture, or a part of it, must be restricted (although rights not only restrict culture; they also protect it, as shown above). The only alternative is to limit rights of people for the sake of the rights of cultures and I think most people would find it unfair it they were obliged to make this kind of sacrifice.

If it is wrong to give the culture of the West an absolute value and to impose it beyond its original territory, then it is equally wrong to give cultural relativism and diversity an absolute value. Cultures and cultural diversity are not the highest values. Other things count as well and may sometimes even override culture. Some cultural practices should not enjoy absolute protection just because they are cultural and just because other cultural practices, that were harmless from the point of view of human rights, were once needlessly attacked by an arrogant, pretentious and imperialistic Western culture. It is not arrogance, pretentiousness, imperialism or Western short-sightedness to condemn mutilation as criminal punishment for example. It is only a judgment on the incompatibility of universal (not Western) human rights standards and certain cultural practices (although one can question whether these practices are really cultural, rather than instruments of power), and on the priority of one or the other. In addition, Western practices as well must be judged in this way, and if this happens consistently, it becomes much harder to denounce rights promotion as imperialism.

Hence, the *reality* of human rights elsewhere in the world depends on the efforts to make rights *real* in one's own part of the world. It also depends on:

- A correct assessment of the importance of diversity compared to the importance of rights.

- A correct understanding of the link between rights and the West, i.e. an understanding that rights are not a Western notion alone and that other cultures are not devoid of the values inherent in rights.

- The realization that the cultural argument is often self interested.

- The relative importance of the individual and his or her culture, and the importance of one for the other.

- Breaking the analogy between rights promotion and colonialism or neo-colonialism.

- A correct understanding of the extent of the modifications of cultures required by human rights and the protection of cultures offered by human rights..

Moreover, it does not have to be an outsider making a judgment on the incompatibility of universal, not Western, human rights standards and certain cultural practices, and on the priority of one or the other. It can and most often is an internal cultural struggle between different and contradictory parts of a culture. People who are the victims of certain cultural practices do not always value these practices higher than a universal ideal or other parts of their culture that reflect this ideal. They do not believe that the adoption of this ideal or the abandonment of certain practices will destroy their culture or alienate them from their culture. They merely want to have a say on the content of their identity and culture. They will reject parts of this content that are incompatible with their belief in human rights. After all, why could not this belief be part of their identity as well? Identity is much more than cultural identity, and belonging is much more than belonging to a culture.

Identity and belonging are important and should be protected, and culture is therefore also important. But other things beside culture are important for identity and belonging. The fact that people all over the world claim their human rights, sometimes against certain aspects of their cultures, but more often against those in power, is perhaps the best argument in favor of universality.

If we want to make rights *real* for everyone, then we have to insist on universality and we have to reject theories like cultural relativism. We have to change certain cultural practices and many more non-cultural practices that are, voluntarily or involuntarily, masquerading as cultural ones. We also have to overcome shame, a typically Western shame nurturing on the pride that once led to colonialism. This shame now leads us to the erroneous belief that different cultures must go their own way, free of meddling and criticism, because anything else would force us to repeat the errors of the past. Our shame hands the individual over to his culture, "his country right or wrong". Instead, we should be proud when defending human rights, proud on perhaps the most glorious achievement of humanity.

THE RELATIVITY OF RELATIVISM

We can safely assume that the cultural criticism of human rights is mainly an instrument in the hands of rulers seeking to maintain their rule. In that case, making rights *real* means that we can simply ignore this criticism or, at most, point out that we are dealing with a self-interested misconception (a conscious or unconscious one), and then apply some form of pressure on these rulers.

But what do we do when the idea of human rights is in contradiction not to the actions of rulers but to widely shared and popular cultural practices, and when many of the victims accept these practices? Female circumcision has been held up as an example of a practice which often leads to serious rights violations (bodily integrity, physical harm, pain), but also religion-based discrimination against women which may be translated into legal punishment for rape victims, for example. Or the caste system in India, which can limit certain persons in their choice of profession. First, we have to state firmly that there can be no trade off. In order to protect human rights completely and fully, we have to criticize and try to change certain cultural practices in order to make them consistent with human rights, and not work the other way around. How can we do this while at the same time respecting the diversity and the equality of cultures and the individual choices of people? How can we combine pluralism and a common opinion on rights?

We should respect and protect identity, culture and diversity as much as possible, but within certain limits determined by the duty to respect human rights as the only true guardians of identity and diversity. If an element of an identity goes beyond these limits and violates human rights, then it must be modified. In all other cases the identity should be considered as a right. And because these other cases will be the majority of cases, the modification or suppression of a relatively small number of cultural practices will not harm diversity and cultures as such.

But why this priority of rights over culture? Why the effort to bring practices in line with rights rather than rights in line with practices? One answer can be found in the fact that human rights protect certain things that are important to people, more important than those aspects of their cultures that violate human rights. When part of a culture has to be modified and we have to convince people to change a certain cultural practice, then part of the answer is that we must try to persuade people that human rights are linked to something they consider more important and valuable than this practice. Elsewhere I have given lengthy arguments linking rights to things like prosperity, peace, etc.[2] The *reality* of rights depends on the success of this persuasion. It also depends on the possibility to convince people that their initial choices for certain detrimental cultural practices are perhaps not really *their* choices but rather the involuntary result of education, tradition, indoctrination, a misunderstanding of the requirements of their religion, or other factors.

Relativism, respect and diversity stop at a certain moment. In any case, relativism cannot be absolute without contradicting itself. If no value is better than another, then relativism itself is not better than another point of view. An absolute relativism would betray its own principles and undermine

---

2 See Spagnoli F. 2003, *Homo Democraticus, On the Universal Desirability and the Not So Universal Possibility of Democracy and Human Rights*, London: Cambridge Scholars Press, for a detailed argument on these links. I cannot repeat this argument here for lack of space. I will, however, give one example in the final chapter.

itself. So relativism is relative itself, and hence limited. However, limiting relativism for the sake of the *reality* of rights does not mean returning to the days of Western supremacy and does not mean judging a culture from the standpoint of another, supposedly superior culture. The standard of judgment is a universal point of view transcending the level of cultures, which is shown by the fact that the culture of the West is also judged and certainly does not always perform better than other cultures when it comes to human rights. So there is a universal point of view transcending relativism. There is more in the world than a collection of equally valuable and separate cultures. Relativism is a useful tool to generate respect for diversity, but we should not bow to the absolute or unconditional plurality of cultures.

Of course, if we want to achieve a common opinion on human rights and recognition of this universal point of view, then we need to engage in intercultural dialogue. This dialogue can be an attempt to convince other people of the importance of human rights and of the link between these rights and some of their cherished values. It can also uncover the implicit presence of human rights in different cultures or the covert motives behind cultural arguments.

This dialogue needs to go both ways and it requires mutual respect. A lack of respect for other people and for the plurality of cultures will inhibit dialogue and therefore also the universal application and *reality* of human rights. A dialogue by definition takes place between equals who respect each other. Nobody is persuaded when one of the parties to the dialogue believes himself to be superior and speaks without listening. No one should believe to be in possession of the truth and of the only correct and just system. Opponents of human rights should also be able to convince proponents.

This equality means that an intercultural dialogue is not a conversation in which one culture needs to convince other cultures, as if some cultures need more convincing than other cultures. Persuasion is a two-way street and at least as much an intra-cultural affair as an inter-cultural one because many attempts to change cultural practices are based on other cultural practices.

However, too much respect for plurality, as can be seen in dogmatic relativism, will also inhibit the universal application of human rights because it will inhibit the necessary transformation of certain cultural practices. Human rights in a world of diversity would be a nice phrase to sum up the necessity of balancing the two important elements of unity and plurality.

Everyone's right to his own culture is very important but is conditional upon respect for human rights. The importance of culture does not diminish the duty to respect human rights.

The intercultural dialogue also has to be a dialogue where there is at least a possibility that one convinces the other. A *dialogue de sourds*, a dialogue of the deaf, cannot create consensus. This means that extreme or absolute relativism is not an option. Cultures have to be allowed to influence each other, to open themselves and to mix with each other. Sealing off cultures and keeping them out of each other's way because of the protection of identities, makes a dialogue impossible. Being persuaded means changing certain elements of one's identity.

The need to convince one another implies a certain degree of tolerance and freedom of expression. It seems as though the conclusion is implicit in the premises. The attempt to universalize human rights through intercultural dialogue already requires the exercise of human rights. You cannot dialogue with someone who is intolerant or who is not allowed to speak his mind.

We should be very clear on one last aspect of this dialogue: it can never be a negotiation. There can be no negotiation on human rights. It is "take it or leave it", even if one can temporarily accept a partial adoption of human rights for strategic and practical reasons. Something is not as good as everything, but it is better than nothing.

CHANGING CULTURES

We have to avoid overestimating the problem. In general, universal human rights are compatible with cultural diversity and even protect this diversity. However, cultural identities can contain elements that violate human rights (even if most violations have non-cultural causes). These elements should not be viewed as expressions of a valuable plurality of cultures. A violation of human rights is not justified because it is part of a culture, because it is very old and traditional or because it has become a habit. Customs, practices, laws and acts of state must in the first place conform to human rights, and not only to traditions, religions or other elements of culture. Something is not good simply because it is old or part of an identity.

One can never deduce a norm from a fact. Habit, conformism or indoctrination through education can make many immoral things acceptable, especially if we can use the authority of culture. But something is not good just because it is accepted. We must be able to criticize and, if appropriate, reject old and traditional habits. We have had anti-Semitism in Europe for ages, but that does not mean that we have to keep it. The moral acceptability of slavery was taken for granted for centuries, but is now universally rejected, including in Islam, for example. So why should it be impossible to reject other elements of Islam or Judaism or Christian cultures?

I think most people would accept that diversity is good and uniformity is bad, but not in an absolute and simplistic sense. How are we to reconcile universal human rights with those cultures that contain elements that restrict human rights? And can we do so in all cases, without inflicting too much harm on either rights or culture? The premise of this book is that human rights should have priority and cultures, rather than rights, should change. However, if people are not convinced of the importance of human rights and of the link between human rights and some of their most cherished values, then they will not change their cultural practices. The *reality* of rights requires that we explain this link and try to persuade as many people as possible. This persuasion will make it possible to change cultures. However, as stated before, I will not elaborate on this here. I just mention the importance of the task without going into a detailed action plan.

The reinterpretation of culture is another requirement for the *reality* of rights. Many cultural arguments for maintaining rights violations are based on only one interpretation of the culture in question, and often an interpretation of a particularly vocal, powerful and self-interested minority. For example, we can challenge misogyny in the dominant religions by using elements from within those traditions. People can be reminded of certain less familiar texts emphasizing the equality of, or respect for, both sexes. Other texts can be put into a historical perspective and can be explained by linking them to historical circumstances. Today's circumstances may require a different emphasis. Texts can be reinterpreted in a more liberal way. Of course, this does not always work. Some texts simply do not allow for a liberal interpretation and others that do are easily counterbalanced by many less liberal texts that cannot be fudged away, because of their supposed divine origin.

The attempt to rephrase human rights in a cultural idiom is another way to reconcile rights and culture and make rights *real*. A notable example is the Universal Islamic Declaration of Human Rights of 1981 in which human rights take on an Islamic vocabulary. This makes it possible to deduce human rights from Islamic traditions. If this works, it can be very successful because it translates human rights into the cultural language of the people. Human rights can only have a real existence if they are respected and applied by the people and if they belong to the fundamental norms and convictions of the people. The problem is that attempts like these often result in reduced versions of the body of human rights. In order to accommodate elements of cultures that are difficult to harmonize with human rights, one often chooses to restrict human rights instead of cultural practices or norms.

There is only one solution to the problem of incompatibility of rights and (parts of) cultures. Somewhere along the line, we have to change cultures and the cultural behavior of people, and we have to do so in a way that respects these cultures. There is nothing wrong with wanting to change cultures. They change anyway. We can and must criticize and change traditions. If not, our lives will be limited to the sterile repetition of the past.

However, it is notoriously difficult to change cultures. The cultural argument seems to oppose change. How can we change what we have to protect and respect? The fact that cultures are often very old or are believed to be very old also inhibits change. People believe that something old must have proven its use. After all, if it were useless, it would not have survived for so long. Fortunately, a cultural identity or a tradition is often, if not always, something artificial. It has been created by man, sometimes in the very recent past, and therefore it can be changed by man.

In the case of female circumcision, for example, it might help to organize some kind of information campaign exposing certain prejudices or misunderstandings regarding fertility, hygiene, etc. or pointing to the fact that neither the Koran nor other Islamic texts prescribe this practice. In addition, one can try to make people conscious of the contradiction between this practice and other values they cherish, such as the right to life and the absence of pain.

A big step forward in the case of religions which create impediments to the full protection of human rights (Islam is but one of them and I would not want to give the impression that Islam is the main problem or is somehow incompatible with human rights), would be to introduce some kind of separation between religion and the state, on the condition that this does not affect the core of the religious identity. The state is often used by a religion as an instrument to violate human rights (and vice versa). We can see this in the case of certain Islamist revolutions, the European Inquisition, or even, although probably less harmful, the way in which the religious right in the US tries to legislate against gay marriage or the teaching of evolution in science classes. However, even the core of religious identities can and does change. The exact nature of this core is constantly being discussed, as far as discussion is possible, of course (Islam provides harsh punishments for heresy and apostasy).

A separation between religion and the state cannot harm a religious and cultural identity. The public domain created by such a separation can function according to its own rules and provides enough space for the expression and conservation of a religious or cultural identity (or various identities, to be correct). However, this kind of separation does make it more difficult to use the power of the state to impose an identity on others. But then again, this seems to be a good thing from the point of view of both human rights and identities, with the exception of those identities that explicitly require their imposition on others.

Culture has to be put in its place, in its place in society, to be more precise, and out of the state. This is the only way we can stop the defenders of culture from taking up the sword of the state. On the other hand, separating the state and society, and confining culture to the latter, is not enough. Human rights can be violated in society without the help of the state (instances of Islamic discrimination against women is an example, although this practice has had a lot of help from states, for example through inheritance laws or education laws). If a cultural identity still violates human rights after the state and society have been separated, then it may be necessary to change some aspects of this identity (through state enforcement of rights for example).

In terms of religion-dictated norms, the biggest obstacle to such a change is the conviction that man cannot change what is given by God. Those who interpret the Bible and the Koran in a literal fashion, construing them to be the word of God, may lead to violations of human rights if some passages are applied and are not counterbalanced by other messages.

In addition to the Koran and the precepts it contains, there is also a body of rules destined for everyday life and developed by Muslim scholars on the basis of the Koran in the three centuries following its creation. Together with the rules of the Koran, they form the Shari'a, the holy Muslim law. The Shari'a, although at first sight a human creation — unlike the Koran, it is not the word of Muhammad, who was believed to be inspired by God, but is an early interpretation of the Koran by his followers — is often considered to be of Godly origin, like the Koran. The Koran and the Shari'a are a sufficient basis for the laws of a Muslim country. At best, human rights or other laws can only play a role when they do not contradict the law of God. At worst, the execution of the law of God is the only legitimate role of the state, even if this implies violating human rights.

The problem is that the Koran as well as the Shari'a often contradict human rights and that changing them is believed to be the same thing as changing the word of God, which is said to be impossible. Human rights advocates can try to convince people that part of the Shari'a is clearly not of Godly origin, not even according to the Muslim faith. That could help to make rights *real* in Muslim societies.

Fortunately, most Muslim states do not or do not completely apply the letter of the Koran and the Shari'a in their laws and actions, and most Muslim citizens as well are not fundamentalists or literalists in this sense. They balance contradictory passages against each other and mix certain elements of Islamic traditions with elements of Western legal traditions as well as local traditions. The Islamist or fundamentalist movements which have appeared during recent decades wish to see the complete (re)introduction of the long neglected laws of the Shari'a and the Koran, although in practice many of the laws of Muslim countries are already inspired by these "original" precepts. Since many of these existing laws already violate human rights, it is clear that changing them to make them more consistent with "traditional" or "correct" Islamic practice would only aggravate the human rights situation.

Human rights proponents should take sides in the internal Islamic discussions between fundamentalists and those Muslims who do not agree that the Shari'a is a God-given law adapted to present day needs or that the Koran should be applied literally.

> The term Shari'a, literally "path" or "way'" . . . did not initially denote a legal code at all. The interpretation of . . . divinely sanctioned material, and its elaboration into a set of comprehensive legal codes, is known as fiq' (literally 'understanding', hence jurisprudence), and it is this, humanly evolved and variously codified, body of legal material that has come to prevail in Muslim society under the, misapplied, term Shari'a. Thus what is today invoked as an unchangeable, and sacred, body of text is, even in Islamic terms, nothing of the sort. As the Syrian writer Aziz al-Azmeh has written: "Islamic law is not a code. This is why the frequently heard call for its 'application' is meaningless, most particularly when calls are made for the application of Shari'a — this last term does not designate law, but is a general term designating good order . . . Calls for the 'application of Islamic

> law' have no connection with the Muslim legal tradition built upon multi-
> vocality, technical competence and the existence of an executive political
> authority that controls the legal system. It is a political slogan, not a return
> to a past reality".[3]

Because the Shari'a is a human artifact and the human interpretation of
the word of God, it can be altered by humans without relinquishing the fundamental core of the Islamic cultural tradition, namely that life should be
organized according to the word of Allah.

Another obstacle to change, often combined with the obstacle of Godly
origin, is the time-honored nature of many practices. Something old must
have proven itself and the wisdom of previous generations must be respected. Fortunately, traditions are not always as traditional as we are led to
believe. Instead of something very old and established, traditions are often
recent creations or highly selective interpretations adapted to present-day
aspirations. The claim of trans-historical and established traditional thought
is often used to justify contemporary thinking. It is useful to mention this
when traditions are used or manipulated in order to justify rights violations.
This will at least eliminate the excuse that violations are old, respectable and
part of an ancient culture.

The culture of the West can be an example of change. It has changed dra-
matically throughout the centuries and it is still changing today. Many of its
supposedly ancient traditions have been adapted or abolished and this has
often been very beneficial from the point of view of human rights. Very few
Westerners wish to return to the practice of slavery, for example, a practice
once considered acceptable and traditional. Most of us see this change as
progress. However, one can only see this as progress and achieve this progress when there is a norm independent of the existing culture, a non-cultural and hence universal norm. This norm is used to judge existing cultural
norms. Because cultural relativism denies the existence of such independent
and universal norms, it inhibits progress.[4] It can only see what is, not what
should or can be.

---

3 Halliday in Beetham, D. 1995, *Politics and Human Rights*, Oxford: Blackwell, p. 160.
4 Cliteur, P.B. 1997, *De filosofie van mensenrechten*, Nijmegen: Ars Aequi Libri, p. 56-7.

Inalienable, Natural and Legal Rights

Human rights protect a number of universally important values such as peace, prosperity, freedom, diversity, identity and belonging,[5] so it is safe to say that human rights are also universally important values, although some convincing still needs to be done regarding the link between these values and rights. If everybody is to enjoy the benefits of these values, then human rights must be applied and respected universally. If human rights protect values that are important for human life as such, wherever it is situated, then we can say that human rights are rights that belong to humanity, just as the values they protect belong to humanity. That is why they are called "human" rights.

If human rights belong to humanity, then they can never be taken away, whatever happens at the political or legal level. In other words, they are in-alienable rights. Of course, the fact that rights cannot be taken away does not mean that they cannot be violated. But people who are tortured still have the right not to be tortured.

Since human rights belong to humanity, all flagrant and structural viola-tions of human rights are crimes against humanity. These violations attack a part of humanity (they attack certain values that are a part of humanity), a part sufficiently important to label an attack on this part an attack on hu-manity. Incidental violations of one particular human right do not necessar-ily make it impossible for the victim to realize the values that are protected by human rights and that are a part of humanity, and are therefore not crimes against humanity (although it can happen that they make it impossible; an incidental violation of the right to life, for example, makes it impossible for the victim to realize all kinds of values). These conclusions may or may not be accepted in legal theory. The point is that I believe they should be.

Human rights are not only inalienable rights but also natural rights (as opposed to legal rights), because they are independent of politics, law and other institutions. In the first instance, human rights are not situated at a political or cultural level, but at a natural level. They belong to all members of a natural species, namely the species of human beings, even if they are not legally recognized. All members of the human species, independently of po-litical or cultural associations, share certain values (peace, prosperity,, etc.) — in the same way as they share certain biological characteristics, for ex-

---

5 See note 2.

ample the ability to walk on two feet (the concept of natural rights is therefore metaphorical) — and should therefore also share the mechanisms necessary to protect these values. The description of how exactly this protection functions is beyond the scope of this book, although a short example will be given in the final chapter.

A human being does not have human rights because he or she happens to be a citizen of a certain state, a member of a certain class or culture or whatever. He or she has human rights because of his or her humanity and because of the values one can associate with humanity. Since being human means having certain values, one can say that every human being, for no other reason than being human, has rights, independently of race, culture, class, state, agreements, laws or whatever. Each man or woman is entitled to human rights by virtue of being born a human being (the word "natural" comes from the Latin word "nasci" which means "being born"), not by virtue of the body politic, the social group or whatever category he or she belongs to.

That is why it is possible to claim that human rights are universal and unconditional. If you have rights for no other reason than the fact that you are human, then all human beings have these rights. Constitutions, declarations, treaties or laws do not grant rights and are not conditions for the existence of rights; they only declare and protect rights and make them enforceable. It is not the existence of but the respect for rights, the *reality* of rights rather than the property of rights, that is dependent on human creativity and human artifacts such as the state, the law, the judicial system, etc. The existence as well as the meaning and content of rights are a simple consequence of humanity.

Human rights are at the same time independent from and dependent on the state. They exist before or above the state and at the same time they can only have *reality* in the state. First, they are

> in sich selbst geltende Normen, welche vor und über jedem politischen Sein gelten, weil sie richtig und vernünftig sind und daher ohne Rücksicht auf die seinsmässige, d.h. positiv-rechtliche Wirklichkeit ein echtes Sollen enthalten,[6]

that is, norms that are valid before and above politics, laws and institutions because they are right, reasonable and necessary independently of the positive, existing legal and political reality.

---

6 Schmitt, C. 1993, *Verfassungslehre*, Berlin: Duncker & Humblot, p. 8-9.

Human rights exist before and above the state; they are not given by the state and cannot be taken away by the state. The state can of course violate them, but violating rights does not make them disappear. On the contrary, this makes them all the more important. They become part of a moral claim. When rights are not violated, they retreat to the background, they are not even noticed and they become, in a certain sense, unimportant.

However, the role of natural rights in moral claims, important as it is, is not enough. Only the state, by way of the constitution, the laws, the judges and the police can effectively guarantee human rights, enforce them and make them *real* (something which cannot always be said of moral claims; power is often more successful than persuasion). We can enforce and therefore enjoy our natural rights only because the state creates and protects legal rights that are legal translations of our natural rights, and because the state gives everybody a legal personality — a legal person is an entity subject to the law and holding legal rights and duties enforceable by a judge — on top of everybody's natural personality (the latter is the basis of the common values that can be used as a justification of human rights).

The state gives a tangible *reality* to our rights because it translates our natural rights into legal rights that can be enforced by an executive and a judicial power. We are not only natural individuals or specimens of a natural species having some common values, but we are also citizens of a state. If we are not recognized as citizens or if we are not granted a legal personality — as, for example, slaves, or "illegal" and "non-uniformed" combatants in the so-called war on terror — then we are outside of the range and the protection of the law and maybe just as powerless as someone who is excluded from humanity. We do have rights — we are human after all — but the law does not recognize our rights and, consequently, we cannot claim our rights in a legal way. We can only claim them in a moral way and we cannot enforce them, except when we can persuade people or when we are strong enough to use force.

> [I]t is not the natural Ego which enters a court of law. It is a right-and-duty-bearing person, created by the law, which appears before the law … the persona, in its original theatrical sense, was the mask affixed to the actor's face by the exigencies of the play; hence, it meant metaphorically the "person", which the law of the land can affix to individuals as well as to groups and corporations.[7]

---

7 Arendt, H. 1990, *On Revolution*, Harmondsworth: Penguin Books, p. 107.

Without "the protecting mask of a legal personality",[8] without legal rights and without citizenship, our natural rights are incomplete and fragile, but they do exist albeit in most cases in an *unreal* way, as words rather than facts, ideas rather than practices. Their *reality* then depends on chance, good will, persuasion or our power to defend ourselves. More often than not, they will be *unreal*, violated, and denied.

So natural rights without legal rights are incomplete, but without natural rights we would only have legal rights, or the rights that the laws would happen to grant us. There would be no independent standard to judge these legal rights. Rights are indeed the children of law (from law come rights), but it is equally true to say that the law is the child of rights because the law serves the protection of rights. The state, the law and the legal person are instruments to protect, enforce and *realize* human rights (they are of course not the only instruments; international law or charity for example are other instruments which I will discuss later on).

The rights of man are always, in the words of Edmund Burke, the "rights of an Englishman".

> The survivors of the extermination camps, the inmates of concentration and internment camps, and even the comparatively happy stateless people could see . . . that the abstract nakedness of being nothing but human was their greatest danger.[9]

To enjoy these rights requires more than being a part of humanity. It requires being a part of a state, being a citizen. That is why it is worthwhile to protect the state. A number of relatively recent phenomena (such as economic globalization, international flight of capital, international crime, ecological problems, etc.) limit the power and the resources of the state. This can lead to a situation in which the laws are powerless and human rights unenforceable. Of course, the state must not be protected in all cases. A powerful state can be as much of a threat to human rights as a powerless one. Only a certain kind of state, a state respectful of human rights — and this can only be a democracy, as I will argue in Chapter 9 — is worthy of protection.

Natural rights are not guaranteed or enforced by nature, but by the state and the law (*point de droit sans Droit*, there are no rights without law). Natural rights require legal rights. However, when the state does not guarantee human rights, when legal rights are incomplete or inadequate, it is important

---

8 Ibidem, p. 108.
9 Arendt, H. 1979, *The Origins of Totalitarianism*, London: Harcourt/Brace, p. 300.

that the existence of natural rights, independent from the state, is recognized because only then can citizens appeal to their state to give them what belongs to them on account of their humanity. Human rights in the guise of natural rights are particularly important in these cases, because then they are all we have.

When human rights are not recognized legally or politically, they are most in danger; and that is precisely when it is most important to have some way to assert one's claim to them.[10] The difference between legal and natural rights has to be maintained, because both types of rights are equally important. Natural rights are available when we have no (or no adequate) legal rights. If we had only legal rights, we would only have the rights recognized by the law, and the law may be insufficient, depending on how and by whom it is established. Natural rights are asserted vis-à-vis the government in an attempt to force it to give us legal rights when these do not exist yet, or even in an attempt to apply existing legal rights.

If we agree that human beings have rights coming from nature (nature defined in a restricted and metaphorical way as the sum of universal or human values, shared by an entire natural species), then we have to reject the theory of positivism. It is wrong to say that the only rights a human being possesses are those given to him or her by the state or by the tradition he or she belongs to. Someone's political or legal status in positive law does not say the last word on his or her rights or duties. There are rights outside of the state and these rights can support claims to limit the state or to change the behavior of the state. Of course, these rights not only limit the state but also become its purpose because the state should, in essence, be a rights protecting entity.

Human rights transcend and precede positive law, but have to be included in it. Positive law should not neglect or contradict human rights. However, if it does, then the citizens for whom the law has not provided or no longer provides human rights can at least invoke their natural rights and claim that the law be changed. We need our natural rights to make our legal rights *real*, just as we need our legal rights to make our natural rights *real*. Only the existence of a higher law, superior to the laws of the state, can give us the possibility to question positive law, to expose injustices in the shape

---

10 Donnelly, J. 1996, *Universal Human Rights in Theory and Practice*, London: Cornell University Press, p. 13.

of the law and to limit and change the actions of the state. Otherwise, something would be wrong only if it opposes the law. We would then be forced to accept the law and the state as being right in every case.

This shows that the higher law, even if it is not always recognized and enforceable in positive law, is of some use. Even if a positive law or an act of government that contradicts the higher law, cannot always be challenged and invalidated in a judicial way — which means that the (legal) injustice remains intact — we can still use the higher law to label the positive law or the act of state morally invalid and illegitimate (as opposed to illegal). And this can have some effect. Higher law that is not translated and incorporated into positive law is not completely useless and is not merely a *possibility* instead of a *reality*, although it is certainly true that invoking a right that is merely moral rather than legal is no guarantee for success. The fact remains that injustices — for example, injustices translated into a positive law — can only be recognized as such and counteracted if there is a higher law. No law is worth anything if it contradicts the higher law and every law gets its power and authority from the higher law that it is supposed to serve.

The struggle against violations of human rights — whether legal or illegal violations — or, in other words, the struggle for the *reality* of human rights, may require different things, ranging from a revolution or a war of independence in the most extreme cases to rhetorical or moral claims of higher law in other cases. In an ideal democracy, a court procedure is enough. A democratic state can correct itself because it functions on the basis of the separation of powers. Rhetoric or moral claims are not even necessary. The judge uses the higher law, incorporated into the constitution, against the legislator or the executive and forces the law or the actions of the executive to be in accordance with the higher law.

Of course, this means that the higher law has become part of positive law in the constitution, a device that allows us to keep the difference between higher and lower law within positive law. Compared to struggle and persuasion, this is the highest degree of *reality* that the higher law can possess. Rights can only be enjoyed in a complete and predictable way if they are part of positive law and a system of separation of powers. In every other situation, they can only be enforced by way of moral claims or physical struggle, and hence they are fragile if we are lucky and mere wishes if we are less fortunate.

I will describe the separation of powers and its effect on human rights in detail in Chapter 7.

The state, although it does not grant rights, has to recognize them and make them *real*. A constitution is the main instrument for recognizing human rights, and many nations' constitutions explicitly guarantee some rights for humans, and not merely rights for citizens. Everybody within the territory of the state, not only the citizens of the state, can then enjoy those human rights protected by the constitution. The courts and the executive are responsible for enforcing these rights. Citizens as well as non-citizens can go to court and challenge unjust laws or acts of state.

Many democratic constitutions protect the rights of all humans as human beings — or at least those present on the territory of the state — and not just the rights of citizens. The legal rights included in the constitution refer to natural rights as their origin because they are general norms addressing themselves to all human beings, except of course those human beings outside of the territory and the jurisdiction of the state. It would be difficult to try to protect the rights of people who are not within a given state's jurisdiction; this is properly the responsibility of their own state and intervening in the business of other states subverts the idea of sovereignty, risking conflict.

However, some states do attempt to do this as part of a growing effort to see rights extended more and more broadly. In Belgium, some Palestinian victims of the Sabra and Chatilla massacre started court proceedings against the Israeli PM of the time, Ariel Sharon, on the basis of a law on crimes against humanity. Belgium is, of course, unable to prevent future massacres of the same kind, and probably also would be unable to punish Sharon — except symbolically — if he had been found guilty.[11] However, this kind of legislation and trial (based on the principle of universal jurisdiction) is not entirely useless because it sends a signal that humanity does not remain silent in the face of atrocities, no matter how far away they take place. It is a signal of global solidarity. A state can also use non-legal actions, such as international pressure or development aid, in order to attempt to enforce the rights of people outside of its territory. A national judicial system for local purposes and used to aid citizens or people who happen to be on its terri-

---

11 The trial was suspended amid international uproar.

tory, is not the only instrument a state can use to make rights *real*. I will come back to this in Chapter 10.

We can call this latter tool the constitutional universality of rights, not to be confused with the moral universality because it is a universality within a territory, a universal application of rights on all people within this territory. This, however, is not a rule for all types of rights. Political rights for example are an exception because these rights are legitimately reserved for citizens only. A well-functioning democratic state guarantees only the "freedom rights" of all persons within its territory, irrespective of their nationality, not the political rights.

The persons thus covered include of course the citizens of the state (those people having acquired the nationality of the state by birth, naturalization, etc.), but also immigrants, refugees, stateless people, visitors, tourists, etc. The state is an instrument of the law and not an instrument of the nation or the nationality. The nation or ethnicity is not more important than the law. The International Covenant on Civil and Political Rights states the following:

> Each State Party to the present Covenant undertakes to respect and to ensure to all individuals within its territory and subject to its jurisdiction the rights recognized in the present Covenant, without distinction of any kind, such as race, color, sex, language, religion, political or other opinion, national or social origin, property, birth or other status.

Although political rights are also part of this treaty, it is common (and I think also fair) to claim that they may be excluded from this rule and that their use may be limited to citizens. This means that people only have political rights in the state of which they are citizens (in the hypothesis that all states are democracies). This in no way limits the universality of political rights. Everybody has political rights, but not everywhere.

Furthermore, it must be possible to grant citizenship and the political rights connected to it in a selective way, otherwise the distinction would become meaningless. And this is also what happens in reality. There are four good reasons for selectivity in granting citizenship:

1. A definition of citizenship purely based on the physical presence within a territory would be too vague. People could enter and leave the community of citizens all of the time and this would create a permanent state of flux in the size, image and identity of the political community. This would endanger the stability and the permanence of the state and would allow passing

residents to help shape the future of people whose future they do not intend to share. It would therefore be contrary to the ideal of self control and self government that is central to political rights.

2. Political rights and citizenship cannot be exercised effectively if the people do not speak a common language (not necessarily their native language). There is no deliberation and persuasion without mutual understanding and there is no common will without persuasion. A common will is a requirement for the effective use of political rights (more about this in Chapter 9). On top of that, political rights require that the participants in political life know the political system, the political culture, the candidates and the issues at stake. All these conditions for the effective use of political rights and hence for citizenship and nationality seem to imply a further condition, namely a certain stability of residence. It is therefore normal to decide a request for naturalization on the basis of these conditions. However, these conditions do not imply the rejection of multiculturalism. The common language does not have to be the native language and it is possible, in many cases, to know and practice other political and cultural customs without denying one's own customs.

3. Non-citizens usually do not pay taxes. As political decisions often deal with the way in which tax money should be spent, it seems fair to exclude those who do not contribute to that sum of money. Why should you be allowed to decide what is done with someone else's money?

4. If too many poor and unskilled people are allowed into a country and become its citizens, the influx can endanger the country's economic prosperity. This is not egoism. Economic ruin does not help anybody.

These four reasons are all based on human rights. The first reason limits the political rights of transient residents for the sake of the political rights of the permanent residents. (We will see in Chapter 3 how rights can be legitimately limited). The second reason deals with the impossibility of exercising political rights when certain kinds of knowledge are absent. The third reason limits political rights for the sake of the right to property, and the fourth reason for the sake of economic rights. One can only limit political rights (or limit rights *tout court*) when these rights are impossible to exercise because of the absence of certain prerequisites (such as knowledge), or when they endanger other rights. Other reasons for limiting political rights — for example supposed threats to the national identity — do not seem to be legitimate or justifiable.

Something comparable can be said of economic rights. These rights can also be granted in a limited way to non-citizens, and the limits may be less strict than in the case of political rights. Non-citizens who have acquired stable residence as well as non-citizens who have not who but are clearly in need, have an equally valid claim to enjoy economic rights. However, it seems preposterous to allow tourists, other wealthy visitors or even less fortunate passers-by to enjoy the provisions of social security for example. Non-citizens can only expect economic rights under certain conditions. Only freedom rights are constitutionally universal and come with no strings attached. Citizens and non-citizens alike have freedom rights everywhere. Freedom rights are the rights of everybody in all places. All other types of rights are to some extent national rights or rights of citizens only. This does not contradict the principle of the universality of human rights because everybody is a citizen somewhere, or rather everybody has a right to be a citizen of his or her own state. I will come back to this in a moment.

Because everybody is not always or cannot always be in his or her own state, and because political and economic rights are necessary for some important human values such as economic justice, freedom and self government — human values means the values of non-citizens as well — we should try to limit the conditions for the enjoyment of these rights by non-citizens to what is absolutely necessary. Foreigners who know the language, the political system and the general culture, who pay taxes and who have lived a certain time in the country should be allowed to enjoy political and economic rights, even when they are not citizens in the sense of having asked and acquired the nationality of the country. Not doing so would be discrimination, and would lead to frustration and resentment.

CITIZENSHIP AND ASYLUM

However, even if we limit the preconditions to what is absolutely necessary, we will never be able to allow everybody to enjoy all political and economic rights in all states, which would be ludicrous anyway. It is nonsense to try to participate in the common life of every nation or to try to enjoy social security in every state simultaneously. Political participation and enjoyment of public benefits in one state is enough for everyone.

This, however, presupposes the existence of a right to nationality or citizenship (see article 15 of the Universal Declaration of Human Rights). Every person should have the right to be a citizen of his or her state and no state should be allowed to take away citizenship without good reason. This makes it easier to accept restrictions on political and economic rights in other states. Again, these restrictions do not in anyway contradict the principle of the universality of human rights. Everybody possesses all human rights, but not all human rights in all places.

The right to belong to humanity is not enough. We also have the right to belong to a state. Being human and nothing else can be quite dangerous because it means giving up the power to enforce your rights and in particular your political and economic rights. Your nationality or citizenship, the recognition by a state of you as one of its citizens, is of the greatest importance for these rights. It gives you the possibility to enjoy public benefits if necessary, to participate in the government of your country, and, if need be, to enforce these benefits and this participation in a court of justice. You do not have to be a citizen of a certain country in order to be able to enforce your freedom rights in that country, at least if it is a democratic country. In other countries, you may need your citizenship for all your rights, and perhaps you may need a lot more to make all your rights *real*.

The right to citizenship implies that your state cannot take away your citizenship or nationality. It cannot make you a stateless person because that would mean taking away your political and economic rights, and probably your freedom rights as well, albeit indirectly. All types of human rights are connected as we will see later on, and the loss of one type inevitably means the loss of all other types. As a stateless person, you also run the risk of deportation, of being banned from your home and country. The possibility of going to another country as a refugee — even if you are not deported — and of enjoying your freedom rights in that country — if it is a democratic state — may not make up for the loss of your home.

You can, of course, whether you are a stateless person or not, try to acquire citizenship or nationality in another country, where you then also (re)establish your political and economic rights. If you fulfill certain conditions — the four mentioned above — this other state should grant you citizenship. (However, I am not aware of a recognized right to naturalization; there is a right to change nationality — see article 15 of the Universal Declaration of Human Rights — but it is not clear whether the latter includes the former). This may be acceptable from the point of view of the refugee or deportee. Losing your home may be a price you are willing to pay for the protection of your rights, but ideally your original state should respect your right to citizenship together with your other rights, hence removing the necessity to flee.

What can also make it acceptable is that changing your nationality does not mean changing your culture. Learning a language does not mean forgetting another one. And the four conditions for the granting of citizenship do not include the requirement to change culture, religion or ideology. Foreigners seeking to acquire a nationality do not have to assimilate. On the contrary, human rights explicitly protect cultural identity and diversity. People have to be accepted in other societies, within certain limits. The surface of the earth is limited and we have to tolerate other people in our neighborhood. It seems true to say that the earth is everybody's property and that nobody can claim a certain piece of it at the expense of someone else.

Political rights, and to a lesser degree also economic rights, are mainly rights of citizens. The Nazis took away the nationality and the citizenship of Jews, and felons in America forfeit most citizenship rights. Stateless people lose their rights, at first their political rights and afterwards other rights, because of the interdependence of rights. Stateless people are outcasts, without a place in the world, without a community, without the necessary papers to find a job, without the political power or the representation necessary to claim their rights and so on. The right to citizenship is therefore necessary to make other rights *real*, and not only because citizenship offers legal personality and access to courts.

Stateless people and others who can only escape rights violations by fleeing their country must be accepted in other countries. They have a general right to asylum (which is not the same thing as the right to naturalization) and they should not be returned to the country they are fleeing ("Everyone has the right to seek and to enjoy in other countries asylum from persecution", article 14 of the Universal Declaration of Human Rights).

The right to asylum protects people from all violations of rights in their country of origin and, if the country of destination is a democracy, it guarantees the enjoyment of at least their freedom rights in that country. If the asylum seekers are allowed to work in the country of destination — and it is difficult to see why they should not be allowed to work — then they will probably also be able to enjoy their economic rights. Because they work, they will pay taxes, they will learn the language, and they will consider the option of staying in the country. All this will make it easier for them to apply for naturalization and to (re)acquire their political rights as well. This, together with the right to citizenship, is an example of the way in which all types of rights are interconnected and enforce each other. Perhaps the main tools to make rights *real*, are other rights.

This leads to the question whether economic refugees should be given asylum. In principle, I think they should. Poverty is just as much a violation of human rights as is torture. This does not mean that all economic refugees should be able to enjoy social protection the day they arrive. As mentioned above, a state can ask that some conditions be fulfilled before granting social protection. And because it is useless to let poor people enter without giving them economic protection, a state can limit the number of people it allows to enter.

This is a matter of economic efficiency. Unrestricted economic asylum does not seem to be possible. Flooding rich countries with millions or even billions of economic refugees will not help anybody. It will destroy economic welfare in the few places where it exists, without offering any real improvement to the disadvantaged.

The right to citizenship and the right to asylum are human rights in the same way as, for example, the right to free speech. The only difference is that they are second level rights, rights that are necessary to *realize* other rights. Like most other rights, they are not absolute and they can be limited (see Chapter 3). Citizenship can be granted conditionally. And a state is no longer obliged to grant asylum if the applicants are so numerous that accepting all of them would lead to chaos and economic problems in the receiving country. Accepting them anyway would mean sacrificing the rights of the people of the receiving country without being able to do much in favor of the rights of the refugees. It is up to the international community to solve refugee problems. It is unfair to place the burden of accepting refugees on one or a few countries only (often neighboring countries). Besides, combating human rights violations in the country of origin is the best way to solve refugee problems. Most people do not want to flee, so accepting them as refugees is not the best solution from their point of view, even though it is still better than not accepting them.

The state and its parts (municipalities, regions, etc.) are still the most important if not the only possible stage for the *realization* of political rights, mainly because of problems of scale and because of errors in the construction of international institutions. In addition, the state is the best instrument to protect our human rights in general because its judicial and executive powers are most developed. The international judiciary is still in its infancy, not to mention the international executive. The loss of citizenship — an official loss or a de facto loss as a consequence of deportation or exile — is a threat to our rights because citizenship makes the link between our rights and enforcement agencies. That is why there is also a right prohibiting deportation ("Everyone has the right to leave any country, including his own, and to return to his country", article 13 of the Universal Declaration of Human Rights). This again is a second level right, a right necessary for the *realization* of all other rights.

Because of the importance of the state, the simple and rather romantic principle of the equality of all human beings is insufficient. This kind of equality is important because it is the foundation of human rights (the equality of basic values mentioned before), but it can never be the foundation of a state.[12] It eliminates every difference, including the borders between states. And without borders, there is no state. Because we need states, there has to be some kind of difference between groups of human beings as well as some kind of exclusion — not deportation — of certain groups of human beings. We can, for example, exclude people and hence establish states by not granting political rights to strangers, by introducing certain conditions for citizenship, etc.

In addition to the concept of humanity, we need the concept of the people, a people being a part of humanity different from the rest of humanity (not necessarily different in a cultural sense; the wish to live together can be a sufficient cause of difference).

Both concepts, humanity and the people, are equally important for human rights and democracy. Humanity is the justification of universal human rights, including political rights. The people, on the other hand, are the foundation of the state as:

---

12 Schmitt, op. cit., p. 226.

- An institution capable of enforcing our rights in general; and

- A stage on which a people as a separate group of persons can enjoy their political rights and determine their own fate.

By "the people" we mean a group of persons, a separated and different part of humanity that excludes outsiders — within the reasonable limits mentioned above — and that creates a state, a political unity of the people, a political system for the protection of rights and in which the members of the group wish to spend, regulate and control their common lives. Belonging to all of humanity as an equal and undifferentiated whole is not enough. We have to belong to a people, a limited group of persons wishing to live together in one political system.[13] This is dictated by the need to enforce rights and by the ideal of democratic self control. Human rights and democracy require the division of humanity into different groups or different peoples and to some extent determine the way in which this division has to be executed. Democracy requires a common language, for example. They also exclude certain ways. Although it is perfectly legitimate to define a people as a group sharing for example a cultural identity, it would be immoral to exclude people from citizenship because they threaten the local identity. This adversarial attitude often results from the ideology of cultural identity and is unacceptable because it leads to violations rather than the protection of human rights (ethnic cleansing, deportation, rejection of asylum, etc.). Too much attention to cultural identity makes it less easy to grant nationality or entry-rights to strangers, because granting this can be seen as a threat to cultural identity. If we make it too difficult to grant nationality or entry, then we harm rights instead of protecting them.

A definition of a people as a group sharing certain objective characteristics (cultural characteristics for example) also harms rights if it forces the people who share the characteristics to live together, even if they wish not to. Many of the wars between France and Germany were caused by the desire of the German state to incorporate German-speaking French nationals in the German Reich, even when these people preferred to stay in France. This kind of coercion is of course anti-democratic, and therefore it would

---

13 Ibidem, p. 227.

be contradictory to use it as a basis of a state. A state is necessary precisely for democracy and human rights. It is of course possible — but not desirable — to use racism, cultural equality, necessity as opposed to will, etc. as foundations for a people and a state, but it is not possible to use these elements as foundations for a democratic state that respects human rights.

Without the division of humanity in different groups, there can be no state and therefore no human rights (the international community and international institutions are too weak and too far away in order to be able to protect the rights of all of humanity). Political rights in particular cannot function without a state. However, the other extreme, neglecting the unity of humanity, will also harm human rights. This neglect will not make it impossible to have different states and different peoples, but it will make it very difficult to have democratic states that respect human rights because the justification of human rights (our common values that are protected by these rights) gets lost.

The division of humanity into different groups is a kind of exclusion, and unfortunately this has become a dirty word. But it would be impossible to have different groups if all non-members of a group were not excluded. Making a change of nationality conditional and limiting the enjoyment of political rights to citizens of the state is one way to exclude people. Without this kind of exclusion, there would be no groups, no people, no state, no democracy and no human rights. If everybody can belong to one state, without conditions, then there is no state.

However, if the criteria for exclusion and citizenship are too stringent or not relevant, or if citizenship is arbitrarily denied or withdrawn, then it is impossible to have a democratic state (many residents will then be excluded from self government) and to respect the human rights of all human beings. People who flee oppression or rights violations will then not be admitted or will, if admitted, be denied citizenship; and people who are denied citizenship lose, in the first instance, their political rights and, consequently, all their other rights, on account of the interdependence of rights. We will now take a closer look at this interdependence.

Economic Rights = Oxymoron?

The very idea of human rights, and the policy of extending and guaranteeing such rights, as self evidently desirable as they may be, are in fact a vast complex of potentially contradictory principles, ambiguities, questions of degree, and outright oxymorons. Resolving or finding compromise solutions for those problems is a task that governments and international bodies will continue to struggle over for years to come.

Universality or equality is but one characteristic of human rights. Diversity is another. There are many different types of rights, as was already apparent from the discussion in the previous chapter. Traditionally, there has been a focus on freedom rights or civil rights, such as the freedom of opinion or the freedom of thought, but we also have political rights and, more controversially, economic rights. The importance of the right to food, work, housing, social security, healthcare, etc. is a matter of dispute, even among the most convinced proponents of human rights. Champions of the free market say that economic rights are useless, a contradiction in terms, and even harmful because they require a powerful state that would violate our freedom (rights such as the right to privacy and property) in order to protect our economic rights. It will ultimately also harm our economic rights because of the tax burdens it places on businesses and other creators of wealth. They believe that only freedom rights are important and will automatically bring about economic justice.

Some governments of developing countries on the other hand (the Chinese government, for example) believe that economic rights are the overwhelming priority and can even require and justify violations of other types of rights. I will argue that both positions are wrong and that all types of rights are equally important. My argument will be based on the interdependence of all types of rights, another important characteristic of human rights and one which is particularly relevant to the subject of the *reality* of rights. If rights are interdependent, then the reality of some rights depends on respect for other rights. The interdependence of different rights is a general characteristic of all rights, but in this chapter I will focus on one example only, namely the interdependence of economic and freedom rights. In Chapter 9 I will discuss another example, namely the interdependence of political and freedom rights.

Let us start with what we may call the business argument against economic rights. This argument questions whether it is justified to use the word "rights" in the context of economic rights such as the right not to suffer poverty. Are these rights comparable to classical freedom rights or are they an example of the way in which superficial reasoning destroys the meaning of words? Are they rights or are they mere aspirations or desires masquerading as rights?

The claim that the expression "economic rights" is an oxymoron is based on the following reasoning. Rights have to be enforceable. There is no right without a remedy. If a right is violated, then it must be possible to redress the situation in a court of justice. It has to be possible to find somebody who is responsible for the violation and who can stop the violation. If nobody can be forced to respect a right because nobody has the power and duty to respect it, then it is useless and wrong to speak about a right.

Take for example the imaginary "right" to have a climate in which the sun always shines and in which the temperature is constantly between 25 and 27 degrees Celsius. This can be a desire but it can never be a right because it is not enforceable. There is no remedy if it is violated; there is no way to redress the violation. A court of justice cannot decide that the government should take action to *realize* this so-called right. Nobody is responsible for a violation and nobody can stop such a violation. Nobody can be forced to respect the right because nobody has the power to respect it, and hence there is no right.

It is not uncommon to hear the same kind of reasoning in the case of economic rights, although in international law these rights enjoy a similar level of protection as classical freedom rights or civil rights.[1] What we do in the case of a violation of classical rights — ask a judge to force the violator, for example the government, to respect our rights and stop the violation — is often impossible in the case of economic rights. If there is no work, then a judge cannot force the government to give us jobs. If there is no money, then a government cannot have the duty and responsibility to provide social security services and thereby eliminate poverty. "Ought" implies "can". The rule that we should not impose a duty on someone who is unable to fulfill it does not pose any problem in the case of freedom rights. If the government violates our right to free speech, then a judge should be able to oblige the government to protect our right; this protection only requires that the government stop its actions that block us from speaking. It is easy to stop doing something. The moral requirement, the "ought", is always justified when it merely implies the absence of actions.

This criticism of economic rights is based on an exaggerated distinction between the duty of forbearance and the duty of active protection. It is true that freedom rights often require forbearance and economic rights active involvement and commitment, and that forbearance is something that everyone always "can" demonstrate — which is not true of commitment. But things can also be the other way around. All types of human rights depend on judicial and police institutions that in turn depend on the protection and involvement of the state. Even a right such as free speech requires not only forbearance but also the active involvement of the judiciary and hence the state in order to be protected. If our right to free speech is violated, then we may need the help of a judge and perhaps even the police in order to force

1 The International Bill of Human Rights, which is almost universally accepted as the international standard of human rights, contains both types of rights. The Universal Declaration of Human Rights (not really part of international law, but a mere "declaration", although perhaps part of international common law), the International Covenant on Civil and Political Rights and the International Covenant on Economic, Social and Cultural Rights together form the Bill of Rights. The two Covenants are legal documents (treaties) established in order to protect freedom rights and economic rights respectively, and to give legal force to the Universal Declaration that already contained the two types of rights.

the violator to stop his actions. And for some states, it can be just as difficult to fulfill their duty to provide efficient judiciaries and police forces as it is to fulfill their duty to provide work and social security.

If the protection of freedom rights requires as much active involvement as forbearance, then the same is true for certain economic rights. The right to food in an amount sufficient for survival is often better secured by government forbearance than by government action. Look for example at the Great Leap Forward and its disastrous consequences for the people of China, or many disasters in Africa which were the consequences of government action rather than inaction.

All types of human rights are protected or promoted by actions as well as by forbearance. According to the circumstances, a right can be more or less positive or negative. The right to food in Mao's China was relatively negative and if asserted it would be asserted against state intervention. In many inner cities today, it is relatively positive and directed against the passivity of the state.[2] All human rights require both intervention and abstention in order to become *real*. And it is, therefore, unfair to dismiss economic rights on the grounds that they impose duties on the government that are fundamentally different from the duties imposed by "real" rights.

Human rights in general are more than just a means to obtain state forbearance or protective tools directed against the harmful actions of the state. They are part of the state and the state must actively protect them. "That to secure these rights, governments are instituted among men," says the American Declaration of Independence of 1776. In other words, to guarantee human rights is the "raison d'être" of the state. Of course, the state or some part of it can and often does also violate rights, and protection against the state is therefore an important function of human rights and should not be neglected. But it is the state that protects our rights against the state. (International protection of human rights is still mostly ineffective). Power corrupts and that is why we need rights to limit power. However, without power or the state, rights are useless and mere words. Human rights limit the actions of the state, determine what a state is not allowed to do or should refrain from doing, and define those areas where the state is not allowed to interfere. But human rights also, and positively, determine what the state should do. They demand positive action and intervention from the state. In many cases, but

---

2 See also Donnelly, op. cit., p. 33.

certainly not in all cases, this intervention takes place in another part of the state, because many rights violations are caused by the state. Hence, human rights require the separation of powers if we want them to be *real* human rights that are more than just words.

Human rights, all types of human rights, require "le droit à la résistance et à la défense" just as well as "le droit à l'obtention et à l'exigence". We use rights to defend ourselves and to claim help. For example: the state should avoid torturing its citizens and we need human rights to defend ourselves against state torture. If necessary, the judiciary should help us and force the police to stop torturing citizens. This means that forbearance is not enough; the state should also actively protect and help those citizens who are tortured, either by some part of the state or by fellow citizens, and we need human rights to claim and obtain this active protection from the state. There is not a lot of difference with economic rights: the state should not only avoid creating or maintaining poverty, it should also try to create a minimum level of equal prosperity for all, for example by way of redistribution of wealth.

The state should not only forbear but also act in order to make rights *real*. It has a duty to act. And when human rights require that the state abstains, the state should be actively engaged in enforcing this abstention. Every human right, not only the "modern" ones such as economic rights, but also those rights that primarily demand the absence of government intervention, require government intervention, for example intervention in the form of a judgment of a court of justice concerning an illegal government intervention, and the police measures enforcing this kind of judgment. The state should commit as well as omit, and prevent, provide, protect and engender as well as forbear.

The state, and primarily the justice system and the police, protect us against violations of rights. We only have *real* rights, rights that are more than words, thanks to the state. Human rights are therefore not only or even mainly anti-state, directed against the state, and intended to protect us against the state. Something merely negative, such as abstention, forbearance or a limited state, can never constitute a state, because then it would be better to have no state at all. There is a reason for having a state. The essence of a state can "never be derived from something which is a mere negative, i.e., constitutional limited government".[3] Only something positive, such as the protection of human rights, can be the essence and purpose of a state.

It follows that a state that does nothing, violates rights. "[E]st un ennemi de la liberté celui qui non seulement s'élève contre elle, mais ne fait rien pour elle".[4] A state that does not create or maintain the judicial structures necessary for enforcing human rights or the legal and administrative structures for managing social security for example, violates rights, just as much as a state that tortures its citizens or takes away their food and houses.

Consequently, the state cannot fulfill its duty to act if it is not allowed to collect a sufficient amount of tax revenues. Rights, or better the institutions required to make them *real*, cost money, and therefore there are no rights without taxes. Globalization, company relocation, tax evasion, etc. threaten the power of the state and therefore also the effectiveness of human rights. Without taxes, the state can do nothing at all. In view of the role the state has to play in the protection of human rights, globalization can therefore be considered as very dangerous, although it may be beneficial on other levels. (I will come back to it in Chapter 10).

The claim that economic rights are not really rights at all cannot be based on the argument that economic rights require a completely different kind of obligation compared to freedom rights, because such an argument is false. We see that the obligations or duties imposed by both types of rights are essentially the same, although it may be true that economic rights in general require more intervention than abstention, and vice versa for freedom rights. But this is a matter of degree, not of essence. This leads to the *prima facie* conclusion that economic rights are rights and not just aspirations; rights, moreover, that are equivalent to freedom rights.

This equivalence is also supported by the theory of the interdependence of different types of rights. Here I can only give a short description of the way in which such a theory could be developed.[5] Freedom rights need economic rights in order to function adequately. It is obvious that freedom of speech, political participation, freedom of movement, etc. can only be exercised in a

---

3 Arendt 1990, op. cit., p. 147.
4 Mourgeon, J. 1996, *Les droits de l'homme*, Paris: PUF, p. 91. "An enemy of freedom is not only he who acts against it, but also he who does nothing for it".
5 I have tried to construct this theory in more detail in *Homo Democraticus*, op. cit., especially in Parts One and Two.

meaningful way — can only become *real* — when some (if not all) economic rights are respected. Later on in this chapter, I will argue that the opposite is also true: lasting respect for economic rights requires some measure of respect for freedom rights and political rights. This interdependence also gives a *prima facie* advantage to those who claim that economic rights are rights like any other rights.

In any case, if we accept that economic rights are real rights like all other rights, then we assist those who struggle against poverty. They have a right to some relief of poverty. Their claims are not just wishes but rights. Accepting economic rights means encouraging the poor and justifying or legitimizing their struggle. They have rights they can claim. They do not have to beg.

HIERARCHY OF RESPONSIBILITY

Both abstention and protection are required for all types of rights. And these two types of duties are not only state duties. Fellow citizens as well should avoid actions that harm the rights — all types of rights — of other citizens, and should, in addition and when possible, act in a positive way to protect the rights of others. For example, they should not only avoid taking a life, but also save a life when possible. They should not only avoid actions that make people poor, but also assist poor people. They should assist when possible, because "ought" implies "can", also for individuals. If you cannot do something, then you cannot have the moral or legal duty to do it. If you cannot swim, then you cannot have the duty to enter the water to save a person from drowning. If you do not have enough financial means of your own then you cannot be expected to share these means with others who need them too, perhaps even more than you do.

This leads to the conclusion that the opposite rule is also valid: "can" also implies "ought", because those with more power tend to have more responsibilities. If you have invented a life-saving drug, then the human rights of those who can be saved by your drug impose on you the obligation to deliver it. You have a wider obligation than someone who does not have some particular knowledge of medicine because you can do more than such a person.

Rights are equal for all and forbearance is an equal obligation for all, states and individuals, powerful ones and less powerful ones. But active involvement is an obligation that comes in degrees. Our individual and active duties arising from economic rights are not the same vis-à-vis everyone. In general, we have more active duties towards certain persons than towards other persons. Our own children, for example, take precedence. Closeness (in every sense) usually means that we can do more for someone, and if we can do more, we ought to do more. Closeness, therefore, plays a part in the degree of duty, although not in the existence of duty. If we can help more people, then we have some obligation to help more. This is especially the case for wealthy groups — for example, a wealthy country or a group of wealthy countries — that can help many people and maybe even everybody. Consequently, our duties are potentially of a global nature, notwithstanding the importance of closeness.

Real human rights, and especially *real* economic rights, require both responsible governments and responsible citizens, aware of their duties and willing and able to act accordingly. All human rights are rights "erga omnes". Everybody has rights towards everybody else. And everybody has the duty to respect everybody else's rights. Citizens may find it relatively easy to respect the rights of fellow-citizens in the case of rights such as the freedom of expression, because forbearance is in most cases enough. (It is the state which has to go beyond forbearance.) In the case of economic rights, citizens' duties are often more substantial. Forbearance is no longer enough and active help is required. This may explain why these rights are less popular and still actively opposed by many, although not by those who need them.

The possibility to fulfill a duty is a very important factor in establishing responsibility. This means that those who cannot, should not, and those who can do more, should do more. Wealthy individuals and wealthy countries should do more because they have more means to assist. They have no problems satisfying their basic needs; they even have more than is necessary and can easily do without a part of this surplus. Assistance is a duty, not a choice, and people have a right to assistance — within certain parameters.

On the other hand, assistance should not become the rule. If possible, people should be self supporting and independent. Your first duty is a duty to yourself. Dependence can be comfortable, but it is incompatible with freedom and autonomy. If freedom and autonomy mean anything to you, then you should try to be self supporting. Our duties towards other people come into play only when these people have tried and failed to be self supporting. One can be too serious about duties. Assistance can lead to a mentality of dependence and laziness. It can also be seen as paternalism, a lack of respect and unnecessary interference. Therefore, those who need assistance because they can no longer help themselves should be guided towards independence. Assistance is an option only if and as long as independence is impossible. We should try to create the circumstances in which people can satisfy their own basic needs (or at least we should not destroy these circumstances) and economic rights are necessary only when we fail to do this.

When economic rights dictate a need for support, they do so first in a face-to-face situation and then — on a larger geographical scale — in a situation where one person should help other and more distant persons (if the surplus is large enough). Only if all this fails can the state intervene. Duty is a bottom-up affair. Economic rights should not be viewed as primarily the business of the state, otherwise we will lose both the benefits of self support (i.e. autonomy) and of the community spirit that results from spontaneous mutual assistance. Allowing economic rights to be *realized* at the level of citizens' relationships will strengthen feelings of belonging. The fact that our economic rights are realized in part by our responsible fellow citizens enhances community feelings and again supports the statement that human rights are not individualistic and do not only deal with the relationship between citizens and the state. Focusing too much on the duties of the state will create a mentality of passive reliance on government support (for yourself and for others) and a mentality of dependence ("state help kills self help"). Egoism, isolation, irresponsibility and helplessness will become the main features of society. We will only have rights and no duties, rights moreover that only the government should respect and *realize*. In order to avoid this, people should be allowed to act responsibly. They should be responsible for themselves and for others, and the state should not take away this responsibility without good reason (for example the responsibility of parents to care for their children or the responsibility of individuals to find a job).

The state is responsible for fulfilling economic rights only if everything else fails. Only those who are helpless and who have been forgotten by private philanthropy can call on the state for assistance. In this case, the state does not abstain or does not make laws that forbid something; it executes policies that result in an equal supply of those goods and services necessary for the satisfaction of basic needs. These policies are mainly taxation, redistribution and development aid and can be seen as the enforcement of citizens' duties. When the state forces you to pay taxes, it forces you to fulfill your duties arising from the economic rights of your fellow citizens (which is why tax fraud is a particularly reprehensible crime: the existence of taxes is already a stain on the reputation of mankind, because taxes exist as a consequence of the fact that people deny their responsibilities). It is the duty of the state to force people to fulfill their duties, their duty to be self supporting if possible and their duties towards each other if necessary. Government policies of this kind are commands and not prohibitions. But the same kind of commands exists in the field of freedom rights. For example, most municipal law systems contain an individual obligation to save the life of a person in danger, and they punish a lack of respect for this obligation ("failure to assist persons in need").

Big State

This hierarchy of duties allows us to reject a kind of criticism of economic rights that is closely linked to the criticism based on the supposedly different nature of the obligations inherent in economic rights. If economic rights entail obligations of active involvement rather than passive forbearance (contrary to freedom rights, we are told), then one has to reject economic rights because they cause an unacceptable increase in the size and power of the state and a corresponding and equally unacceptable reduction of freedom. A state that wants to protect economic rights has to build an enormous administrative machinery to provide benefits and it has to invade people's private lives (it has to check their income, family situation, the state of their health, etc.).

This reduction of freedom is unacceptable as such, but it also supposedly defeats the purpose. An oversized state hinders the private economy and therefore hinders the creation of the very prosperity that it wants to redistribute in order to protect economic rights. It follows that economic rights are harmful because they lead to the exact opposite of what they want to achieve and because some other values such as freedom are sacrificed along the way.

However, this argument is not as strong as it seems if the *realization* of economic rights is primarily the responsibility of citizens rather than the state. Economic rights can even counter the tendency of a state to increase its size and power. People whose economic rights are *realized* are in a position that allows them to resist illegitimate usurpation of power.

Of course, to be fair, the "big state" criticism of economic rights does not imply a neglect of the problems caused by poverty. It merely states that economic rights and state activity for the protection of economic rights are useless and counterproductive. A fair distribution of prosperity is supposed to follow automatically from freedom. Only free trade and the involuntary actions of the private sector can guarantee economic rights, not the actions of government. The latter will lead to unacceptable burdens on business and private initiative and will therefore undermine rather than promote economic rights because they will undermine the private creation of prosperity.

This quasi-automatic economic justice — reminiscent of the Invisible Hand theory — functions as follows. Free trade, deregulated markets and minimum taxes will allow profits to increase. These profits will then be invested and these investments will increase economic productivity, will create jobs, and will therefore also redistribute prosperity. If low taxes lead to large profits and large profits lead to an increase in prosperity and growth, then this will benefit the poor because they will have a job and an income. All boats rise on a rising tide. Those making large profits will not only invest in production units and in labor; they will also spend money on consumption, which again creates jobs and profits for "small" people. Furthermore, some measure of inequality is an encouragement to do well economically, because doing well economically is rewarded in an unequal society. Inequality therefore leads to economic growth, which then benefits everyone in the way described above. Government grants and social security, on the other hand, lead to passivity and hence destroy productivity, growth and ultimately justice. In the end, there will be nothing left to redistribute.

According to this view, there is no reason for state intervention in the economy or for redistribution of wealth, not even for private philanthropy, and hence there is no need for economic rights. The state, looking for measures to promote economic rights, thwarts the free actions of businesses because it imposes heavy administrative and financial burdens on businesses, making it impossible for them to create and distribute prosperity. There is no reason to have rights. Everything will happen automatically. The requirements contained in these rights will be *realized* involuntarily.

Between the lines of the big state criticism, one can read the story of the age-old struggle between freedom and equality. But it is wrong to depict the struggle for economic rights as a struggle of equality against freedom. Freedom does not have to be sacrificed in the pursuit of economic rights, not if the hierarchy of duties described above is kept in mind. It is not even equality that is at stake in economic rights. Of course, the purpose of economic rights is the equal distribution of the material goods necessary for survival in a decent way. And in order to achieve such a distribution, some things have to be taken away from the rich who no longer have the freedom to do what they like with everything they own. However, the problem that economic rights try to address is not that there is inequality or that some people have more than others or have too much of something. The problem is that some people do not have enough of certain necessities.[6] Everything beyond these necessities can very well be unequally distributed without causing any rights violations.

Those who accept the importance of economic rights do not defend a policy that equalizes all material resources. The policy they defend is one that guarantees a minimum of material means and protection to all people and that uses economic rights to achieve this. This minimum protection is necessary not only for decent survival but also for a meaningful and equal cultural and political life and for the *real* enjoyment of other types of human rights. Public communication and political participation are impossible if all efforts go into the struggle to survive. A certain level of detachment from the urgencies and necessities of nature, from basic biological needs and from the struggle to survive, and a certain predictable supply of food, a house, good health, etc. are prerequisites for human rights, culture and politics.

The purpose of economic rights is the equal possession of a minimum supply of those fundamental material means that are necessary for the continuation of life in a decent way and for a meaningful culture and political democracy. If there are some people who have less than the minimum and others do not redistribute part of their resources voluntarily, then the state using economic rights will redistribute. In other words, these rights will take some things away from those who have enough and give it to those who do not have enough. This is possible because, globally or even nationally in some cases, there is enough for everybody. The only problem is the unequal distribution. The purpose of economic rights is not to try to increase the total supply of the material means of existence. Furthermore, their goal is a necessary minimum instead of a possible maximum; a decent way to survive instead of

---

6 Kekes, J. 1999, *Against Liberalism*, London: Cornell University Press, p. 97.

a life of comfort and luxury; things that are essential rather than things that are merely desirable; basic needs rather than frivolous extravagancies.

Everything that can be added to the equal possession of the necessary minimum can be unequal and falls outside of the competence of economic rights. These rights deal with the basic needs of the poor, not with the fact that some people are rich. However, wealth can perhaps influence political life even when economic rights are respected. Unequal wealth does not necessarily imply disrespect for economic rights, but it can prevent equal participation in political life. Rich people can benefit more from democratic political life than people who are neither rich nor poor. Differences in resources can distort the democratic process because they may distort the will of the people. Therefore, it seems that some kind of redistribution on top of the redistribution necessary for a decent life is a prerequisite for political equality and a true democracy. One can think of rules on political campaign financing, subsidies for political parties, public information campaigns, subsidized education, etc. Such measures can limit the influence on decision-making of the money, the views and interests of leading donors. Democracy, popular sovereignty and equal political participation are also human rights which, if they are to be made real, must be protected against the corrupting influence of unequal resources. I will discuss democracy in detail in Chapter 9.

I agree that the requirement of (limited) economic equality inherent in economic rights (limited equality because only necessities must be equally distributed) imposes a limit on the freedom of some (the freedom of some to do as they like with some of their goods). In this sense it is correct to see economic rights as part of the struggle between freedom and equality. But rights sometimes limit other rights. The system of human rights is not a harmonious whole. Rights often have to be balanced against each other and in certain cases some rights can be given priority over other rights. Take also the example of the privacy of public figures and the freedom of the press. The same is true for economic rights and freedom rights (see also Chapter 3 for a more elaborate discussion of the limits of rights).

The big state criticism can also be attacked because of its naïve belief in economic mechanisms. It is wrong to believe that the *reality* of the economic rights of all individuals follows automatically from unhindered and unintentional economic activity. The benefits of growth do not "trickle down" automatically to all persons who have a right to these benefits, and will not do so even in the naïve utopia where social privileges are abolished and a level playing field of equal opportunities or equal starting positions is guaranteed. Even then will the natural lottery always leave some people in unacceptable situations, because of misfortune or lack of talent or ability or application.

But, of course, the opponents of the big state do not even accept that equal starting positions are created. That would entail a massive attack on property rights. And if the situation at the outset is unequal, then free economic activity will only worsen the situation of the poor. The rich will profit more from freedom and growth than the poor. They have the education and the relationships, and they have the means to invest and to profit from the laws of economics. They will improve their situation, in most cases at the expense of the poor. "If the initial distribution in a trading situation is unequal, the result of trade will be similarly unequal".[7]

I admit that business has to play a part in the *realization* of economic rights, just like everybody else. However, it will not always do so involuntarily and automatically as a consequence of its normal activities, i.e. profit-making. It has to be conscious of its moral duties and act accordingly. If it fails to act morally, the state has to intervene, has to redistribute what is not redistributed voluntarily or automatically, and has to limit some freedom rights for this purpose. Of course, some things do indeed "trickle down" automatically (more flourishing businesses means more jobs for instance), although this is probably not enough to compensate for the many things "trickling up" (for example the "surplus-value" created by workers and expropriated by entrepreneurs who pay the workers only a part of the value that the workers create, or the extra benefits yielded by an already privileged position).

A free market can indeed help to *realize* economic rights, whereas an oversized state can harm economic development and can therefore diminish the prosperity that must be redistributed. However, freedom is not enough, as is proven by experience. The policies of Reagan and Thatcher promoting the free market and trickle down economics have led to social catastrophes. Economic rights, citizen philanthropy and state activity for the *realization* of these rights are necessary. The state must intervene when free trade, trickle down economics, individual responsibility, etc. fail, and the state needs economic rights as the norms of its intervention or as standards of achievement.

---

7 Nelson, W.N. 1980, *On Justifying Democracy*, London: Routledge and Kegan, p. 84.

How?

However, something remains unresolved. We know who has the duty to respect our economic rights (everyone). We even know that there is a hierarchy among those who have a duty and that we have more duties towards some than towards others (those who can do more should do more). We know what kind of duties we have (forbearance and active involvement). And we know of a way in which these duties cannot be fulfilled, at least not completely (the free market). What is still relatively unclear is how these duties can be fulfilled. What should we do precisely? I have spoken about mutual assistance, caritas and redistribution. But what if there is nothing or not enough to redistribute? What if most people are poor and unable to assist others?

I come back to the question of the beginning of this chapter: what if there are no jobs available? Is it useful in that case to ask a judge to give us work? Are we dealing here with aspirations rather than rights, after all? First, most of the violations of economic rights are not the consequence of insufficient resources but the consequence of an unjust distribution of resources, in which case economic rights can be applied immediately, even by way of judicial judgment forcing people to redistribute.

However, what can we do if this is not the case and if there really is a problem of insufficient resources, for example in some developing countries? Let us not forget that in many countries, it is just as useless to ask a judge to enforce our right to free speech, but no one will claim that in this case there is no right to free speech. *Realizing* rights, turning words into facts, is often a difficult matter, and this may be true for all types of rights, including economic rights.

Secondly, if the problem is not one of distribution but one of resources, then this is only apparent. While governments cannot have a duty to do things that they cannot do and cannot be forced to do things for which they do not have the resources — this lack of resources is the case in many developing countries — the problem is still one of distribution rather than the existence of resources once you take a global point of view. International redistribution can then solve the problem. Globally, there are enough resources to eliminate poverty altogether. If a single state is unable to eliminate poverty in its territory, then the same hierarchy as described above comes into play. Self support is not possible, and thus there has to be mutual assistance to achieve respect for economic rights. Other states or the international community have to help. Governments do not only have duties towards their own citizens and citizens do not only have duties towards their fellow citizens. Development aid, if necessary based on taxation, is one way to fulfill international duties, although voluntary assistance and measures leading to self support are again preferable, for the same reasons as those mentioned above. These measures are preferable, but probably insufficient. One can be too naïve about moral motivation and about involuntary and automatic systems.

"Suprema Lex"?

At the other end of the political spectrum, one can find those who do not reject economic rights but instead embrace them as the supreme political value. All other values, including freedom rights, have to be sacrificed if this is deemed necessary for the protection of economic rights. This is the ideology of the current Chinese leadership for instance. However, the economic rights of all citizens can only become *real* in a democracy that protects the "classical" freedom rights and political rights, because economic rights depend on freedom rights and political rights. Freedom of opinion may seem useless when you have to struggle to survive. Economic rights then seem all-important and most urgent, but the struggle to survive cannot be settled if, at the same time, one does not have classical rights as a means to enforce economic rights. Classical human rights and democracy make it possible to show, challenge and change economic injustices. You can express and hence *realize* claims for the protection of economic rights if your freedom rights are respected and if you can engage in democratic politics.

The squeaky hinge gets the oil. Only in a democratic society in which freedom rights and political rights are protected, can an economic injustice be exposed and can claims for its abolition be heard and implemented. People can use rights to demand that fellow-citizens, the government or the international community fulfill their duties and perhaps implement certain economic policies. Most governments, including democratic governments, act only when they are put under pressure. The freedom of expression, the freedom of assembly and association (associations such as pressure groups, labor unions or political parties) and the right to choose your own representatives are instruments in the hands of the economically disadvantaged. They can use their rights and the democratic procedures in order to influence economic and social policy.

Poverty must have a voice. It is true that without a minimum degree of prosperity, human rights and democracy lose a lot of their value. If you have to struggle to survive, then you do not have the time to form an opinion, let alone express it. "Primum vivere, deinde philosophari"; first you make sure you live, and only then can you "philosophize". In a situation of poverty, it is indeed difficult to use rights and democracy, but without rights and democracy it is much more difficult to fight poverty. Not only rights are interdependent. Rights and democracy are also interdependent. I will elaborate this in Chapter Nine.

Economic rights need democracy and classical rights because if there are no free flows of information, no accountable government that needs to justify its actions in order to be re-elected, and no free press, then you may not see the problem and you are also more likely to have corruption, embezzlement of public funds and other "taxes on prosperity". The rule of law, freedom and the openness of government, which are typical of a democracy, limit not only corruption but also the ineffective management or outright squandering of natural or other resources by untouchable governments. Furthermore, there is a link between corruption and squandering. Corrupt governments will be more inclined to set up grandiose but foolish and wasteful mega-projects, because this gives them more opportunities for corruption. Corruption is also a tax on investment, which is why it hampers investment and economic growth. Especially the often all-important foreign investments (the import of technology and knowledge) decrease as corruption increases. All this is detrimental for economic rights.

Economic rights of course promote classical rights because classical rights are of limited use when you have to struggle to survive. But classical rights can also promote economic rights. Both types of rights need each other, strengthen each other, are dependent on each other and are necessary conditions for each other. The full use of classical rights requires the *realization* of economic rights, and vice versa. It is therefore nonsense to say that one type of rights should be sacrificed for another type, even if this is only temporary. Third world governments that believe that freedom should be sacrificed for economic rights will end up with nothing. But sometimes that is of course the real purpose. Freedom rights and democracy are not a luxury that poor countries cannot afford ("first economic development and only then freedom"). They are a bare necessity.

Of course, freedom does not automatically produce economic justice. It is probably a necessary but insufficient condition, insufficient because otherwise economic rights would not be necessary. And there are also benevolent dictators who try to do their best economically and have economic justice in mind. But as long as the poor and the victims cannot express themselves freely and elect their own representatives, their self-appointed leaders will always rely on what they think the people need, not what they really need.

Freedom rights and democracy may be a bare necessity, but the economic situation can be such that they come under serious pressure or that even basic respect for them is impossible. They do indeed require the presence of certain necessary conditions, for example a minimum level of economic development. But wherever they are possible, if only partly, they have to be used to the full and they should certainly not be limited on the grounds of some misguided ideas about priorities. Economic development cannot be a justification for rights violations, no more so than cultural identity. The reason for this is not only the importance of human rights and democracy, but also economic justice, which is highly dependent on rights and democracy.

When thinking about economic rights, one must try to occupy a position between two extremes. These two extremes roughly correspond to the traditional distinction between right and left in politics. The right believes that economic rights are nonsense, an oxymoron, a misuse of the word "rights", useless at best, harmful to the economy and to economic justice at worst. Forbearance, freedom, the free market, the invisible hand, trickle down economics, etc. are the best and only measures to fight poverty. No moral or legal obligations should be imposed on either the state or the citizens. This has been tried extensively and history has shown that it is wrong. The trend, rather, is toward a concentration of wealth in fewer and fewer hands.

The left on the other hand tends to focus too much on economic rights, often at the expense of freedom rights but ultimately also at the expense of economic rights (because of the interdependence of rights). The big state is not a false problem and it is often tempting to violate freedom rights in an attempt to protect economic rights. However, freedom rights are perhaps the most useful means to protect economic rights, and vice versa.

Chapter 3. Limited Rights

Balancing Rights

After this example of the interdependence of rights we should now focus on another characteristic of human rights, namely the fact that they are not absolute, at least not most of them. Even though they are important, they can be limited. Some rights can cause violations of other rights or of the rights of others, which is why rights have to be balanced against each other. The *reality* of some rights depends on limits on other rights.

In specific instances of rights that come into conflict — for example the right to free speech and the right to privacy — a judgment has to be made about the priority of one right or the other. The decision can be made by a judge, but also by the legislator. There can be laws that limit one right for the sake of another. The phrasing of human rights articles in constitutions and treaties often provides the possibility of such legal limits. The abuse of rights with the purpose of overthrowing a rights protecting democracy can also be a legitimate reason to limit rights. Limiting rights for the sake of some other value does not seem to be justifiable.

These limits are an almost daily occurrence, even in a perfect system. The system of human rights is not a coherent and harmonious whole (this is an intriguing and perhaps contradictory complement to the previously mentioned principle of interdependence of rights). Libel or expressions of racial hatred, for instance, are often illegal, and with good reason. Expressions of hatred are not only insulting (people should be able to live with insults); they can also lead to discrimination or even physical harm. It is a thin line between aggressive words and aggressive actions.

The problem of course is how to decide between rights. On what grounds do we give priority to one right or the other? Only if we have a rule for this can we distinguish between legitimate and illegitimate limits on rights, or better between limits and violations. Part of the rule could be that some rights are clearly absolute. It seems unacceptable to kill someone, even if doing so would allow us to protect some other right of some other person. Limits on the right to life will then never be legitimate and this right should always have priority and can in turn limit other rights.

However, this rule leaves most problems of conflicts between rights unsolved because most rights are not absolute. One cannot always avoid moral, philosophical and hence contestable reasoning when taking a decision between rights. Some subjective judgment on the harm we would inflict when limiting one right or the other might help. In the case of a journalist who divulges intimate details about the private life of an actor, what would be the harm inflicted on the journalist when we limit his or her right to free speech? Probably less then the harm he or she inflicts when limiting the right to privacy of the actor. Again, a judgment may not always be as easy as in this example. Deciding between rights remains a difficult matter and one that is better left to professional judges.

Some other decision rules may help. For example, it is evident that limits must remain the exception. So he or she who wants limits must make clear that they are necessary for a particular case and that no other measures short of limiting rights can provide the same result. And limits can only be necessary for the protection of other rights or the rights of others. No other reasons are a priori valid. Decisions on limits must also be justified and argued. One has to make a case and show:

•That limits are in fact necessary (there is a difference between racial hate in an obscure magazine and in front of the gates of a refugee center; probably no harm will be done by the first expression and limits on rights are not necessary)

- That there is no other, less far reaching solution (such as mediation, withholding subsidies or state contributions to party finances)

- That the choice made between rights is the best possible one.

But even when there is no other solution and one needs a law to limit certain rights of certain persons, this will not always be enough. Making the use of a right in a certain way a criminal act is not always enough to make that use go away. Racism, for example, will not disappear by making racists shut up. The underdog effect may even make them stronger. One should also try to do something about the causes of racism (poverty, education, etc.). Making rights *real* does not only require the suppression of those who use rights against rights. It also requires the identification and elimination of the reasons why these people use rights against rights. Healing the symptoms but not the disease is inefficient, but some symptoms are so bad that something must be done, without losing sight of the causes of the symptoms.

When limiting rights it is always useful to remember that rights are means and not goals. They serve to protect universal human values as stated before. Like all means, they can fail to function adequately in certain circumstances. A conflict between rights can then be solved by looking at which of the two rights serves the purpose of rights best in the given circumstances.

LIMITING THE NUMBER OF RIGHTS

The number of different rights also requires some limitation. We have to allow the appearance of new rights, but at the same time we have to recognize that the system of human rights is not served by the limitless production of new rights. Rights lose their strength and power if anything can become a right. *Real* human rights necessarily require some kind of brake on the production of new rights. The fact that people start to call some demand or need a "right" testifies of the strength of the concept — they rightly believe that this will enhance the chances of getting what they want, because rights create duties — but they may do more harm than good if they succeed in convincing others.

The proliferation of rights, the constant talk of rights violations in countries that do reasonably well in the domain of rights, and the continuous expansion of the field of application of human rights (expansion both of the number of rights and of the number of meanings of rights), all this is just as dangerous as outright attacks on human rights. Human rights that lose their content because of overuse are just as *unreal* as rights that are violated.

If everything is a right, then nothing is a right. If every wish becomes a right, then rights decay into wishes. If everything becomes a right, then rights cease to be enforceable and it becomes correct to dismiss rights talk as mere rhetoric, which in turn is very useful for those who violate rights. Important things can no longer be distinguished from unimportant ones ("the right to choose" is the slogan of the American publicity lobby, as if freedom of expression is the same thing as an advertisement, or the right to have an abortion the same thing as the right to buy a Mercedes rather than a Lexus).

An example of the logic that tends toward an increase in the number of rights: why should animals or nature not have rights? Humans are not the center of the universe, something so special that only they can have rights. If both smart and stupid people have rights, why not "stupid" animals?

I admit that people can and do harm animals and nature, and I do not want to minimize these problems. But apart from the fact that the protection of nature can be framed in and justified by the language of strictly "human" rights (the *reality* of human rights requires a world in which we can live, and hence requires the protection of nature), the solution of the very real problems of animals and nature does not require the invention of new rights. There are other ways to solve these problems. One can make the case that we simply have a moral duty to respect animals and nature. However, duties are less popular than rights and hence the temptation to use the language of rights. However, using this language outside of the sphere of humanity means multiplying the risks that I have identified above and that are linked to the proliferation of rights.

I would therefore recommend to limit the concept of rights to humans and, moreover, to some aspects only of human life. Humans are more than a more organized form of slime. They are special. Contrary to nature and other creatures, we are not entirely determined by natural forces. We have specific needs that justify specific protection mechanisms. This human monopoly of rights is not based on some ideology of human supremacy, but on difference. Man is not a purely natural being like other beings, and this specificity is precisely what rights try to protect. Human rights emerge from our specific nature, our humanity. This can even be said of economic rights, which at first sight merely fulfill our natural needs. One could say that they do so in order to allow our other rights to protect our other needs. Freedom rights can be quite *unreal* and useless without economic rights.

It is wrong to gloss over the differences between humans and other creatures. There are certainly similarities, even with the least developed creatures: the ability to feel pain is an important one. And it is often because of pain that people want to give rights to animals. But human rights do much more than defend us against pain. They do so only in order to make other things possible (identity, relationships, communication, independence, etc.). No human would be content with an existence that is merely characterized by the absence of pain.

All this is perfectly compatible with respect for the rest of creation and does not imply some kind of human supremacy. It is often said that respect for human rights and respect for nature do not mix. Excessive freedom and hence human rights are supposed to be the main causes of environmental problems. I am convinced, however, that this is not true, at least not if we can maintain a limited definition of human rights. Environmental problems are caused by industrialization, misguided agricultural policies, over-consumption, indifference, etc. Whereas over-consumption can be a case of excessive freedom, it is hard to see how it could be caused by the provision of human rights. There is, as yet, no right to consume and human rights do not stand in the way of certain limitations on consumption.

Let us also not forget that rights cost money. The more rights we have, the less money we can spend on each one. If we say that a couple that has difficulty begetting a child has a "right" to have a child, then the effort to *realize* this right may cost a lot in comparison with the cost for saving starving children in Africa.

New rights also create new duties for those who have to respect these new rights. Is it not likely that there is a certain level above which it becomes difficult for people to shoulder their duties? And is it not unfair to force people above this threshold? Moreover, states that habitually violate human rights can use the number of human rights as a convenient excuse, and perhaps not without good reason. If there are many rights, then there are many duties, and some of these states can point to a lack of resources. "We cannot do all at once; give us time; first things first; the West has also taken its time to *realize* all rights", etc. It is in the interest of rights violators that the number of rights increases and that, consequently, the significance of the concept of "rights" diminishes.

But rights can also create duties for those who hold the rights. Take the example of two prisoners who claim the "right" to marry and have sexual intercourse. What happens with the baby? Rights can cause problems for the rights of others (e.g. your own children or children far away), as we have seen before. Multiplying the number of rights means multiplying these problems.

There are already enough rights violations, so let us first try to enforce respect for existing rights, before creating new rights and hence new violations. However, new rights may become necessary. Again, the middle ground, now between excessive conservatism and the exaggerated creation of new rights, seems to be the best position.

The rhetorical power of the concept of "rights" is not the only reason why there is an increase in the number of rights. This increase also has something to do with the fact that we now better understand that rights are not only negative but also positive. They require forbearance but also action, intervention and help. Claiming a right is a cry for help, because people now understand that rights are there to help and not just to enforce abstention. We owe more to others than forbearance, but we do not necessarily owe what someone happens to call a right. And if demands are unsuccessful, the "rights" that express these demands are then turned against the state that must take over the "duties" that the rest of us reject. If the number of "rights" is too important, then the expectations are overstretched (we see in the West that the state struggles with an excess of popular demands), and disillusionment is the result. And we all know how dangerous disillusionment can be.

Chapter 4. Individual Rights and Equal Rights

Individual or Collective Rights?

Another characteristic of human rights is that they are individual rights. Every individual has his or her rights. These rights are general, universal and equal and not the specific rights of certain groups. However, could it not be useful, in certain circumstances, to recognize some specific rights of a particular group, in addition to the mainstream and equally shared individual rights? A minority, a nationality, a race or a gender could need certain rights that are its own and that no other group can have. This group may be the victim of a particular kind of injustice. No other group can or ever will be such a victim, and hence there is no need for a general right (for example, women can suffer from a special kind of injustice, an injustice that men will never suffer; the same can be true for indigenous people).

Perhaps, but those who claim that there should be group rights or collective rights often have "normal" injustices in mind, injustices that normal or individual human rights are designed to redress (genocide, political exclusion, religious persecution, discrimination, etc.) but that can be inflicted on entire groups at once. Some rights violators target the individual rights (such as the right to life, bodily integrity, non-discrimination and the freedom of religion) of as many members of a group as possible. This group is a victim precisely because it is a group. The violators think they see certain characteristics of the group that justify, in their eyes, the rights violations. In such cases the only reason the members of the group suffer rights violations is their membership of the group. Jews may be persecuted because they are Jews, immigrants in the US because they come from (or look like they might have come from) Islamic or Arabic countries.

Rights are violated collectively, but these are collective violations of individual rights, not violations of collective rights. It is not because individual rights are violated for an entire group at once that these rights suddenly become collective rights. And it is not clear why collective violations of individual rights should justify the creation of new collective rights, unless one thinks that the protection of collective rights will be more successful than the protection of individual rights. But this is a show of weakness. It is not because the protection of individual rights poses problems that one should abandon these rights and replace them by other rights. One should instead put more effort in individual rights.

Collective problems require a collective solution, it is said. A minority that is collectively oppressed claims a collective right to protection, a collective right not to be oppressed. Acts that are expressed in collectivist terms have to be countered by rights using the same terms.

The question is whether it is really necessary or even opportune to solve the collective problems of some groups by way of collective rights or group rights. I believe that the often genuine problems of different groups and minorities (but also majorities) can be solved by applying a number of individual rights such as the right to equality before the law (a law has to be general and equal for everybody and cannot be directed against or cannot discriminate certain persons or groups), the right to equal treatment and to equal rights, the right not to be discriminated, the right to life (in the case of genocide) and religious liberty.

The problem of gender discrimination in a number of countries is an example of a collective problem that can be solved by applying individual rights. There is no reason to solve this collective problem by adding so-called women's rights or collective rights of women to the existing individual rights. Gender discrimination is not a violation of women's rights. It is a violation of the human rights of women. The principles of equality and non-discrimination are sufficient to solve this problem.

Another example is the economic backwardness of certain minorities, such as black people in certain parts of the USA, workers, single mothers, etc. Applying individual economic rights is sufficient. There is no need to rush into a search for special minority rights, for example the right to positive discrimination or affirmative action (favoring a group deliberately or treating a group deliberately in an unequal yet positive way in order to help it advance and gain a status equal to the rest of the population). Applying positive discrimination is accepting the failure of human rights. If the members of the group are able to enjoy and enforce their individual rights, and if everything is done to achieve this goal, then there is no need for positive discrimination. And when there is a need for positive discrimination, then not because this is a collective right, but because it is a somewhat strong measure to realize individual rights of a certain group of people who, historically, have accumulated a backlog in the protection of their rights.

Individuals can form groups to claim and enforce their rights, just as groups can use individual rights in their defense. It is often necessary to form a group in order to be heard (take for example the feminist movement). However, this is a matter of strategy, not content. Enforcing individual rights through group action does not turn individual rights into collective rights. Individual rights are sufficient in all cases, although I have to admit that protecting groups by way of individual rights ignores or neglects the nature of the problem. Only the right of a group (for example a group of indigenous people) to equal treatment recognizes the existence of a certain kind of discrimination. The individual right to equality, even though it can stop group discrimination if applied effectively, ignores the nature of or the motivation behind the attack on the group and does not distinguish between individual and group discrimination.

However, the advantage of countering a collective attack by way of an individual right is that the existence of individuals in the collectivity is thereby accentuated. The cause of a collective attack is precisely the belief that a group is a collectivity and a unity in which the individuals do not count. By using his or her individual rights to protect a black person against discrimination, racism or genocide, we accentuate his or her individuality. Instead of being "just another nigger", someone belonging to a collectivity which is a supposedly legitimate object of discrimination, he or she reaffirms an individual identity.

Individual rights accentuate the individuality of the person claiming the right, and already hint that there is no reason for discrimination. Discrimination requires collectivities and the absence of individuals. If necessary, those who discriminate create a collectivity ("blacks are lazy; gays are promiscuous, etc."). Recognizing collective rights can contribute to the official sanctioning of reasoning in terms of collectivities. It makes this reasoning legitimate, it puts the different individualities in the background and it strengthens the opinions of those who oppose and persecute certain collectivities.

Another danger of collective rights, especially the right to preserve a group's identity, is the way in which they encourage closed groups. The freedom of association implies not only the right to form, join and maintain a group, but also the right to leave a group, the right to stay outside of a group and the right not to be forced to join or stay in a group (the same is true for the freedom of religion). Membership of a group is a free and non-final choice. This is not an expression of individualism. Communities are a very important part of an individual's life, but not all kinds of communities. Individuals as members of a particular group must be able to decide when this group is no longer important or has become harmful. It is not up to the groups to decide that they are an important part of their members' lives. Individuals decide which groups are important, which groups they wish to join or leave.

The right to leave a group is important because groups can violate the rights of their members. For example, the so-called collective right to identity and the desire to preserve an identity can tempt a group to force its members to express this identity, even when certain members have deviating views. The identity of the group is then more important than the individual identity. This was often the case during the period of de-colonization. The long forgotten national identity was then forced down the throat of every citizen, especially the "évolués". This also happens in some states of the Third World seeking a new and cultural legitimacy now that their anticommunist legitimacy has disappeared. These states often force different ethnic groups in their territory to conform to the national ethnic identity that has become a national ideology. However, it also happens on a much smaller scale, for example a group of youths "worshipping" a certain musical group or following a certain fashion and psychologically forcing some individual members to conform. The collective right to a group identity can encourage this kind of reasoning. If a group has a right to an identity, then the members have a duty to protect and uphold this identity.

Individuals who wish to leave a group because this group violates their rights or forces them to conform, are often forced to stay. The survival and identity of a group is dependent on the presence of members. Individual rights are seen as instruments used by individuals to attack the group and its identity and must be eliminated. This kind of reasoning is particularly harmful when adopted by a state as a means to protect a national identity. An authoritarian form of government is then necessary to suppress views and attitudes deviating from this identity. This is no longer a right to have an identity; it is a duty to have an identity, a cultural identity that forces the individual identity to disappear into the collective. A group must be able to express and preserve its identity, but it should also allow its members to express and preserve their own, individual identities and leave if necessary. And individual rights such as the freedom of religion, of association, of expression, the right to non-discrimination, etc. are sufficient for groups to preserve their identity. No special right to identity is necessary. Such a right could even be harmful to individuals.

Fortunately, forced conformism is becoming more and more difficult to maintain or to impose. Thanks to increased mobility and modern technology, individuals can look outside of their group and can use the outside world against their group. For example, the attempts of certain Islamic countries to ban the Internet and satellite TV can only succeed with the use of extreme force, something that is likely to create a reaction. On top of that, the economy of the country in question will probably suffer from such measures.

The individual should never be subjected to the whole. The identity or even the existence of a group can be put on the line as a consequence of the application of individual rights. Groups are there for individuals and not the other way around. It must be possible to impair or change groups as a result of the application of individual rights. This impairment or change should be kept to a minimum because groups are important for individuals, but the only alternative is harming individual rights in order to protect groups (for example, one can coerce individuals to conform to the group or to remain members of the group). However, this would mean that the individuals exist for the sake of the group rather than the group for the sake of the individuals.

Individuals would view such a group as oppressive. After all, difference is as important for human beings as belonging.

SELF DETERMINATION?

There is yet another problem caused by collective rights: supposing that there are collective rights, which groups have these rights? Take for example the right to self determination: which group has this right, and which does not? In the case of colonies, the answer is clear. Colonies were occupied territories without self government but with clear albeit not always just or sensible borders. The people of this kind of territory had a universally recognized right to self determination. ("A state administering a colony is under a legal duty to allow the inhabitants of that colony to exercise their right of self determination"[1]). The focus here is on the inhabitants of a territory, which is an unequivocal criterion for the attribution of a right.

Today, however, the right to self determination is no longer claimed by colonies but by national minorities of all kinds. A national minority is not as easy to define as a colony. What is a national minority? What is a nation? Who is or is not a member of a nation? Almost every group of a reasonable size can call itself a nation and if the common language does not define the nation or the common identity, then history, race, religion or something else will do. If we give every so-called "people" or "nation" the right to self determination, then we open the gate to all kinds of centrifugal forces. Every excited separatist who calls himself the spokesman of his "people" can claim the right to start a war as the ultimate means to *realize* the right to "national self determination".

Political self determination is said to be necessary to solve certain minority or group problems when individual rights do not seem to protect the interests of all communities in a sufficient way. We have seen in Chapter 1 and we will see again in Chapter 5 how groups can use individual rights, but not everyone is convinced that these rights are enough. It is said that only self determination or life in a separate and independent state can guarantee that minorities or other groups are not discriminated against, are not persecuted, are not economically disadvantaged and can live according to their identity.

However, this implies a lack of belief in the strength of individual human rights. Struggling for political autonomy — just as applying positive

---

1 Akehurst, M. 1991, *A Modern Introduction to International Law*, London: Harper Collins, p. 298

discrimination — means accepting the failure of human rights. I do not mean to say that political autonomy is wrong — there can be no democracy without it — or that it is always wrong for a minority to try to secede. Sometimes, normal institutional protection of human rights within a national framework does indeed fail to work and then there is perhaps no other solution than independence. Only a separate state can then make rights *real*.

However, one should first try to protect human rights within an existing state and only if this fails can one use stronger measures. The risk of violence inherent in secession supports this statement. As the purpose of self determination is a better protection of individual human rights (when normal institutional protection is not available), there can never be a trade-off between self determination and individual rights. The latter always have priority and the goal of self determination cannot be a state that violates rights.

If self determination, political autonomy and secession are sometimes necessary for the *reality* of rights, then this is not because they are collective rights. They are simply means to protect and *realize* individual rights. The state is a rights protecting tool, as stated in Chapter 1. At most, these so-called collective rights are a general wording or rephrasing of the individual right to political participation. Respecting a people's right to self determination is the same thing as respecting their individual political rights because these political rights allow people to determine their own fate, free from internal or external powers that try to determine their common lives. But only individuals have a right to political participation, and it is not because individuals can only exercise this right in common (in groups, movements, parties and nations) that this right automatically becomes a collective right.

However, some say that the right to self determination and the right to a separate state have another use besides the protection of individual rights (including political rights): they protect the cultural identity of a group. It is granted that classical individual rights can guarantee the physical survival of a group. But cultural, religious or ideological destruction, they say, can only be avoided by using the right to self determination. The right to the identity of a group — for example the right to a cultural identity — is then dependent on its right to self determination. No individual right is able to protect a group identity. Only in a state of its own can a cultural group fully protect and develop its identity, speak its own language and live according to its own norms.

This is wrong again. Individual rights guarantee the right to a collective identity. There is no need to rush into self determination. Freedom of expression, religious liberty, non-discrimination, tolerance, local autonomy, etc. create a duty to accept difference. If somebody has the right to express his difference, then we have to accept this difference. Everybody has the right to have another opinion, other norms and values, another religion, another language and so on, with the exception, of course, of the norms, religions, etc. that violate human rights. Individual rights guarantee the existence of different identities as long as these identities do not violate individual rights. The freedom of association permits people to form and join groups with different identities. The individual right to form and join groups implies the right to protect a group as well as the identity of a group. A group without an identity is not a group. Freedom of association is useless if the identity of the association does not have to be respected.

If you believe that an identity can only be protected by way of self determination and the creation of a new state, then you have lost all hope for individual rights in the current state. You may be right, but very often you are wrong and too extreme in your proposed solution. Secession — or revolution, which is also an act of self determination, not in most cases of a minority, but of the majority — can be useful. An identity is after all very important. Living in a community that supports such an identity is part of the good life and must be protected by human rights. If our current state is not able to protect our human rights, then a new one perhaps will. However, it does not follow that we must accept the existence of collective rights.

Most of the new collective rights are in reality existing individual rights disguised as collective rights. For example, the right of a disadvantaged group — e.g. a developing country — to be aided by a wealthier group (the right to development) is just another way of phrasing economic rights. The collective right to self determination is the same thing as the right of a people to choose their government and to participate in the government. The right of a disadvantaged group — e.g. women, people of color or indigenous populations — to equality and equal participation in politics is a combination of political rights and the principle of non-discrimination. Collective rights as such are both superfluous (because they are always a rephrasing of individual rights) and harmful (because they sanction thinking in terms of collectivities rather then persons).

NATIONALISM

Self determination is the essence of nationalism. A nationalist believes that a people or a nation can only have an autonomous and authentic existence, according to their own traditions, values and norms, in a state of their own. Although this does not show much belief in human rights, he or she often sees himself as a force for democracy. Self determination, the national liberation of a nation that is captured in an alien state and that has to follow the decisions of an external power, can indeed be part of the struggle for democracy. As stated before, self determination is another word for democracy.

The difference between a democrat who believes in human rights and a nationalist who believes in national self determination, is that the former accepts diversity within a state. A democrat believes that individual human rights can offer protection of group identity and group rights, and can avoid group persecution, discrimination and unequal treatment. He also believes that the democratic organization of the state offers self determination to both the people of this state as a whole (through political rights) and to the parts of the people (through decentralization, federalism, etc.). A nationalist believes that only a state of their own can give groups what they need. He has lost hope, or never had hope, in human rights or the different democratic forms of participation and self government.

It is obvious that the nationalist desire to have a perfect match between state and nation can cause problems. If every nation, in the sense of a group of people with a separate identity, should have its state, then every state should comprise only one nation. A multicultural nation can never be legitimate according to nationalism, because one assumes that in such a state it is inevitable that some nations or peoples are ruled by others and hence do not have an authentic and autonomous existence.

This is a gross simplification of democratic government. If democracy would be no more than majority rule, then the argument could make sense. The minority, which may be a national minority, would then indeed lose self determination and perhaps even its identity, depending on the measures taken by the majority. But in a real democracy, the majority must respect the human rights of the minority and the organization of government must be federal so as to give self determination to the different parts of the population.

Human rights and democratic government protect identity, authenticity and autonomy. Moreover, the nationalist solution creates an even bigger problem. The policies of nationalism lead to a homogenous society that lacks the benefits of diversity and multiculturalism. Most problems of multiculturalism — a lack of integration, conflicts between communities, one group dominating another — can be solved by rights and democracy (by tolerance, respect for religious freedom and individual rights, non-discrimination, institutional reforms, local autonomy, etc.). Nationalism solves the problems of multiculturalism by destroying it.

It is a kind of intellectual laziness to go immediately for the most extreme solutions. The only way to have homogenous territories in our multicultural and melting-pot world with no clear territorial separation of nations within states is the use of force. Homogenization often requires violent separation, forced relocation of members of other nations, "ethnic cleansing", civil war — because of the violent reaction of relocated groups or of states that want to keep their territory intact — and sometimes even genocide. It also creates centrifugal forces because of a lack of clarity: which group is a "nation" and has therefore a right to its own state? This vagueness encourages all kinds of groups to demand self determination.

If members of another nation have the misfortune of inhabiting parts of a territory that is claimed by the nationalist nation as the soil of its future state, and if these members do not leave the territory, give up their possessions and abandon their graves voluntarily, then nationalism requires the expulsion or even elimination of these people. As long as they are present, the state will not be the representative of one nation. Democracy will require the representation of all nationalities and that is not the optimal situation for nationalists because it means that every single nation is not able to rule itself independently and that some nations may be ruled by others.

Of course, one must accept that multiculturalism and diversity protected by human rights are not always possible. Some problems between groups can become so extreme that living together is no longer acceptable and that normal mechanisms to promote coexistence (tolerance, rights, federalism, etc.) no longer work. Separation may then be the only solution. However, I am convinced that these normal mechanisms, when consistently applied and enforced from the beginning, prevent the escalation of problems. Most ethnic or cultural conflicts take place in authoritarian states or in immature democratic ones. In any case, separation creates new populations that will harbor new conflicts (take the case of Kosovo). So it is better to find ways to deal with conflicts than to try to exclude or deport them.

Separation may not be the best way to solve problems between groups because these problems may not have been caused by cultural factors but by poverty, demagogy, etc. But even if they are, the solution of separation means giving in to the racists. You in fact agree with them: groups should not mix. You could also take the difficult road: do something about the causes of racism and problems between groups, enforce tolerance, create a well-functioning federal system, share resources, etc.

Nationalism and homogenization can also lead to imperialism, even though imperialism contradicts self determination and national liberation. A nationalist state will always be tempted to expand its territory if this is required for the "liberation" of compatriots "annexed" and oppressed by a neighboring state (an idea that caused the war in former Yugoslavia). The fact that these compatriots often have something very different in mind is of no importance (as is shown by the fate of the German-speaking inhabitants of the east of France in the 19th century).

The nationalist assumption that a heterogeneous state is incapable of giving a certain level of freedom and self determination to the nations or cultures that are part of it, is shortsighted and shows a lack of faith in human rights and democracy. Democracy is compatible with federalism and even requires it (political participation can best take place on a local level). If the nations are geographically separated or willing to move and concentrate, then they can use local autonomy in a federalist state to rule themselves to a certain extent, to live according to their own traditions, to speak their own language in their relationships with government, etc. Even if the level of autonomy would be less than in a state of their own — which is not necessarily the case because this state can be a tyranny — then this may be acceptable compared to the dangers and pitfalls of separation. And even if nations are mixed geographically, groups can still be accorded the right to manage certain group affairs on their own. Groups can also use their individual human rights to enforce some level of independence even without any local autonomy, and to protect their members against discrimination.

Finally, nationalists should not be naive about the possible level of autonomy in a state of their own. The time is gone when states were independent. A state of your own does no longer guarantee independence. Everybody becomes more and more dependent on the rest of the world. Some problems require global cooperation rather than national independence. A small state resulting from nationalistic separation may only get a false sense of self control and may have to become part of a larger group after all. All the offers and victims of separation may then have been in vain. I will come back to this in Chapter 10.

A nationalist does not really need human rights. Rights are, after all, a way to manage differences. If you exclude differences and try to create a mono-cultural society, then the usefulness of rights diminishes. Homogenization for nationalists does not only mean mono-culturalism. The individuals inside a nation or a culture are also subject to a kind of homogenization. Individuals are not so much different personalities but rather parts of a culture, specimen. Every culture has its typical personality, its way of life, its way of being human, its national character or "Volksgeist". The personal identity is a collective identity. This cultural identity — Chinese are hard working people, Scandinavians are somewhat to themselves, etc. — influences or even determines the ideas and behavior of the individual members of the culture and is formed by the religion of the nation, its language, history or even the climate. An individual is born in a culture and formed by it, from his earliest years on. He cannot choose another one and cannot reject his collective identity. His life follows certain patterns that are older than him and that will live on after him. Everything that may seem at odds with the collective identity is in fact comparable to the small movements on the surface of the sea that may go in different directions but that cannot escape the underlying current. Like the current, the culture may not always be visible but it does determine everything.

If individuals receive their personality from their environment and culture, then the members of a group share the most basic assumptions and convictions, and then it is indeed likely that a mono-cultural society will have fewer conflicts than a multicultural one. And then it is acceptable to give in to racists. Imperialism is also acceptable because if people belong together, then the mother-country is allowed to occupy parts of neighboring countries inhabited by people of the same nation, whatever these people or their government think about it.

However, all this is based on psychological simplifications. Although it is undeniable that the environment, the group and the past shape our identity, there is no reason to ignore the possibility that individuals free themselves from their immediate environment and tradition. The whole world can influence us and we may choose to be extremely individualistic. Belonging and identifying with a group are important, but so are originality and individuality.

Nationalism is a political and psychological simplification but it is also naive about the chances to reduce conflicts by separating collective identities in different states. Many different things can cause conflicts. It seems that the current fashion to explain international conflicts by way of cultural differences or differences in "civilization" is also a simplification, caused by Islamic terrorism for instances, but also by theories like the one about the "clash of civilizations", although the inventor of the phrase, Samuel Huntington,[2] is more nuanced than many of his followers.

According to this strand of cultural reductionism, the struggle between capitalism-democracy and communism, which was mainly an ideological struggle, is now replaced by the struggle between civilizations or cultures, a struggle no longer based on convictions, ideology or the economy but on identity. The identity of one culture may be threatened by another one, which causes conflicts. The bloody borders between civilizations (in Israel, Serbia, Chechnya, etc.) are given as proof. In order to avoid these conflicts, one has to separate cultures. Multiculturalism, immigration, etc. have to be avoided, and the borders have to be defended militarily. Every nation or civilization should strengthen its identity if it wants to be in a strong position vis-à-vis others.

All this can be true to the extent that culture is the cause of conflict and that rights and federal democracy have proven unsuccessful to deal with these problems. Sometimes this is the case, but often it is not, and then other measures are more adequate. Conflicts between the West and Islam are perhaps in part caused by differences in culture, but probably more so by economic circumstances, the Palestinian problem, etc. In any case, there are just as many conflicts within civilizations or cultures as between them (Rwanda,

---

2 Huntington, S. 1998, *The Clash of Civilizations and the Remaking of World Order*, Simon & Schuster.

Korea). The differences between members of one civilization are often more important than the differences between members of different civilizations.

EQUAL RIGHTS

Although the consequences of nationalism are often unacceptable, some of its initial motivations are based on human rights and democracy. Nationalism is in many cases a struggle for the equal rights and the self determination of an oppressed minority. A basic characteristic of the system of human rights is the belief in the equality of rights. All human beings have the same rights and the rights of all human beings are equally important, wherever they live, whether they believe in a God or not, are rich or poor, or whatever. Human rights are rights of all people at all times.

One can even say that there is a right to have equal rights. Article 2 of the Universal Declaration of Human Rights states that

> Everyone is entitled to all the rights and freedoms set forth in this Declaration, without distinction of any kind, such as race, color, sex, language, religion, political or other opinion, national or social origin, property, birth or other status.

There can be no discrimination in matters of human rights. If everybody has equal rights and if, therefore, nobody should be discriminated against in the use of his or her rights, then human rights are universal.

All people must have equal rights because human rights protect universal values. Everybody has an equal claim on the rights necessary to protect everybody's values. Human rights belong to everybody in an equal way because everybody needs them in an equal way to realize certain values.

It is unacceptable that some people have, for example, the right to free speech and others do not, or only in a limited way. There can be no privileges. No person has more rights than another. Everybody's rights are equally important. In a situation of unequal rights and discrimination, certain people have less opportunity to realize some important values. Of course, someone who considers other values to be more important than prosperity, peace, freedom, equality, etc. can waive his or her rights and can accept inequality. However, it seems to me that this can only be his or her decision. Other people should therefore always respect this person's equal rights.

Equality of rights is a very important principle. In the same way as tolerance (see Chapter 8), it promotes the *reality* of human rights. Equality means the duty not to discriminate when applying human rights, whereas tolerance means the duty not to suppress certain ways of using human rights. The enjoyment or, better, the possibility to enjoy human rights must be equal for everybody. It is unacceptable that some people can enjoy more human rights than others, or can enjoy some human rights more than other people can. That this equality is a right is shown by the fact that most people consider it wrong or consider it an injustice if people are treated in an unequal manner. Equality of rights is of course not always a fact, but it is a right, a right to enjoy all other rights to an equal degree, neither less nor more than all other people. The state can enforce this right to equality, and can make it *reality*.

It is clear that there is a link between equal rights and non-discrimination on the one hand and tolerance on the other hand, even though non-discrimination is concerned with equality and tolerance with freedom (or, better, with the acceptance of freedom). When people are discriminated against and when their rights are taken away or limited, we see that this is often the result of intolerance or unwillingness to accept the particular way in which these people use their rights. The statement that some group has fewer rights than other groups can be based on the conviction that one is allowed to tolerate less from this group. Intolerance leads to discrimination (but not necessarily vice versa).

Historically, the idea of equal rights resulted from the emergence and the ascent of the bourgeoisie and was in the first instance a tool for the protection of their interests. The bourgeoisie was, compared to the aristocracy, a relatively open class. One could enter and leave this class in a relatively free and sudden way and the moment of entering or leaving was sometimes hard to predict. For this reason, it was undesirable to create a new set of privileges in the style of those of the older classes. If the bourgeoisie was to have rights to protect its interests, they had no choice but to instate equal rights for everybody.[3] The final step in the transformation of privileges (or freedoms and rights limited to certain groups such as guilds, corporations, the nobility, etc.) into general or human rights was the taken by the revolutions of the 18th century. From this moment on, human rights were considered to be rights of individuals as entities detached from concrete relationships and groups.

---

3 Donnelly, op. cit., p. 70.

Having equal rights also means having rights vis-à-vis everyone. We have rights "erga omnes". Everybody, states, groups, individuals, have to respect our rights. Every right can be invoked "erga omnes", in relation to everybody. Everybody has a duty to respect our rights. Someone's right is everybody else's duty, although the degree of this duty can differ from person to person (see Chapter Two). Equal rights do not always mean equal duties.

Of course, equality transcends the realm of human rights. There are other important types of equality besides the equality of rights. We consider it wrong and unjust if someone is treated in an unequal manner, whether in the field of human rights or in any other field. According to most people, equality and justice are the same thing, but this is only partially true. Injustice can arise out of an unequal treatment of people that are equal, but also out of an equal treatment of people that are unequal. A pupil, who considers that he earns a higher score than the rest of the class, will feel that he is the victim of an injustice if the teacher gives every pupil the same score. Being just means also giving everybody what he or she deserves to get, not only what he or she has a right to get. Discrimination is not wrong or unjust in every aspect of life. It is unjust when it is applied in certain domains — such as human rights, where desert is irrelevant because human rights are unconditional — or when it is applied according to the wrong criteria — for example the teacher giving scores according to personal preferences instead of merit.

The question is then: when is equality necessary, and when is discrimination acceptable? Discrimination is clearly unacceptable when dealing with human rights. Every inequality is then an injustice. The reason is that, although people are not equal and do not wish to be treated as equals in all aspects of life, they are equal on a certain basic level of humanity and this basic level is the level of the values protected by human rights. That is why people have to be treated equally and have to have equal rights at this basic level.

The case of the criminal may cause a problem. The convicted criminal apparently has fewer human rights than law-abiding citizens, and is treated in an unequal manner. The answer to this is that a criminal is convicted and punished because otherwise he would violate the rights of law-abiding citizens. A system of rights naturally punishes violations of rights — otherwise it would not be able to survive — and this punishment necessarily entails violations or better limitations of rights of the people who are punished. I cannot imagine any punishment which does not entail rights limitations.

Indeed, the solution to the problem lies in the difference between violation and limitation. Everybody's rights are limited, not only those of the criminal. For example, you cannot yell "FIRE!" in a crowd without a reason, because this might lead to violations of the rights of the crowd. People might get trampled as a result of your "free expression". Unlimited rights nearly always provoke violations of other rights, the right to life and bodily integrity in my example. In the same way we have to limit the criminal's right to free movement because otherwise he may violate the rights of other people. Therefore, the criminal is not treated in another way than other people. A citizen in a cramped theater must not yell, "FIRE!" Perhaps he has fewer rights than the citizen on expedition in the Sahara desert. In the same way, we can accept that a criminal, who has killed someone and is locked up for it, has fewer rights than law-abiding citizens.

One might answer that the rights of the criminal are more limited than the rights of law-abiding citizens and that, consequently, there are no equal rights. Even if this is true, it is clear that treating people equally means trying to avoid serious harm done to many people or to an individual in a more rigorous way than less serious harm done to a few people or to an individual. So being more severe to a criminal is in perfect agreement with the principle of equality. Rights should be limited in proportion to the harm they may do to other rights or to the rights of others, otherwise there can be no equal rights.

There is another possible solution to the problem of the rights of a criminal. The right to equal rights can perhaps be limited, just as many other rights and for the same reason as other rights, namely the protection of rights. People should not always be treated equally and should not always have equal rights. Those who violate the equal rights of others — and who therefore create inequality — have to be punished and lose some of their rights. They are treated in an unequal manner and have unequal rights.

Chapter 5. Religious Liberty

Limiting and Separating the State and the Church

Religious liberty or the freedom of belief is a human right. It is the right to be protected against both government and private coercion in matters of religion, to be free to practice and profess a religion of your choice or no religion at all, in private as well as in public. Implicitly it is also the right to change your religion.

Religious liberty is an important value because it counteracts religious persecution and coercion and hence protects diversity, plurality and group identity. It makes a monopoly of one religion impossible — except when culture and demography are such that there is a de facto monopoly that is not contested — and it guarantees the coexistence of different and publicly competing beliefs. In this way, it also guarantees debate and diversity in general. If there is debate and diversity on the level of religion, then why not on other levels? On top of that, religious liberty guarantees tolerance: if people can be tolerant — or are forced to be tolerant — in the field of religion, then they will probably be tolerant in other fields as well.

This shows that religious liberty can be of interest to non-religious persons, not only because it protects them from the imposition of a religious belief, but also because it allows them to live in a world of tolerance and diversity. Religious liberty is therefore an integral part of a democratic society and of a system of human rights that also aims at such a world, and it is further proof of the interdependence of rights.

However, there is a downside to the concept of religious liberty. Anyone can call his or her personal idiosyncrasy or even insanity a religion in order to try to get government protection. There is no easy answer to the question of what is or is not a religion in the proper sense of the word and what therefore merits the protection of the freedom of religion. However, it is obvious that any belief or practice that is part of a religion or claimed to be part of a religion, and that, at the same time, provokes violations of human rights, should not be protected under the right to freedom of religion. Human rights are limited and have to be balanced with other rights. Freedom of religion is no exception. In particular, the right to non-discrimination, although closely connected to religious liberty (one should not be treated badly as a consequence of one's religion), can be a problem if everything can be labeled a religion and if every imaginable theological ideology can enjoy an absolute level of protection. The equal rights of women, for example, should be balanced with the right to practice a religion that provokes discrimination of women. Limiting one right for the sake of another is a normal practice in the field of human rights (see the discussion in Chapter 3).

Religious liberty implies that the state (but not only the state) should not interfere with the religion of its citizens, should not favor or discriminate a particular religion or religions, and should not attach benefits or penalties to any religious affiliation or lack thereof. Religious liberty therefore limits the power of the state and creates a difference between state and society by granting some measure of religious independence to society.

If the state should avoid interfering in religious matters, in an ideal world then it should be neutral as regards religion. There has to be a separation between state and religion (but not necessarily between politics and religion, see later) in the sense that there can be no official state religion. The state should not link itself to a particular religion but should stand above the plurality of different religions. Without this kind of neutrality, certain religions as well as atheists and agnostics will be worse off compared to the adherents of the official or quasi-official religion, if they are allowed to exist at all. By religious liberty I mean to say religious equality and the equal treatment of all religions (— and lack of religion). This equal treatment is impossible if there is some kind of link between the state and a particular religion. If there is no religious equality, if adherence to one religion brings more advantages than adherence to another — and this is very likely to be the case when the former is an official state religion or is in any way favored by the state — then there is no *real* religious liberty. The choice for one religion rather than another will not be a free choice. Even if non-official religions are not actively persecuted or discriminated against, they are worse off when there is no separation between the state and religion because they have less means to influence the public as the official state religion. They are not as free as the official religion.

Another reason why religious liberty implies the separation between state and religion and the religious neutrality of the state is the need for an impartial judge to mediate between different religions. If different religions are allowed to exist together, we need a non-religious law that regulates their coexistence. It is very unlikely that people adhering to one religion will accept laws that are inspired by another religion. The fact that a religiously neutral state with its religiously neutral laws allows many different religions to exist and to coexist, makes it acceptable to many people. A state that only allows one religion, favors one religion or makes its laws on the basis of one religion will only be accepted by the adherents of that particular religion. The historical fact that religious communities tend to become more and more intertwined within the borders of states will enhance the attractiveness of this kind of state.

Just as the state is kept out of religion, religion is kept out of the state. The claims of religion are restricted. A particular religion cannot claim to be the religion of the country in order to take possession of the state or the law and thereby achieve more power than other religions and impose itself on individuals. The state, for its part, is not allowed to prohibit, persecute, discriminate or impose a religion, and it should also avoid using a religion as a means to enhance its authority, as a kind of transcendent confirmation. If you stand close to something glorious, you may hope that something of the glory shines on you as well. You may even hope to become godly, which, historically, has been an enormous advantage to states in pre-modern times. The king, the representative of God on earth, was godly as well, and he who is godly is eternal and escapes contestation, which is of course anti-democratic and incompatible with those human rights that protect democracy.

The state should not interfere with religion, and religion should not interfere with the state ("Give to Caesar what belongs to Caesar and to God what belongs to God"). Power does not come from God and does not have to follow God or render an account to God. Power comes from the people and has to render account to the people. State and religion are mutually independent.

Separating state and religion may cause some problems. It will for example make it more difficult to universalize human rights. Many cultures, for example Muslim cultures, see this separation not as an advantage but as a problem because religion — unified religion, not the freedom of religion — is still very important in their societies and is considered to be the foundation of politics. However, state neutrality in religious matters does not imply that democratic politics is necessarily a-religious or atheistic. A democracy executes the will of the people and not the will of God, but if the people believe that their will equals the will of God, then this does not pose a problem as long as the religious and other rights of the minorities are respected and as long as the religion of the majority does not acquire unjustified privileges and does not become the official state religion.

The problem is rather that the majority does not always execute the will of God as everyone understands it. A religious person must always follow his religious opinions, no matter what the majority decides, and therefore cannot always respect the will of the majority. God does not accept to be in the minority or to be overruled by the majority. A religious person can only accept democracy when he or she happens to agree with the majority. I will come back to this and I will argue that such a person can have other reasons to accept democracy, even if this democracy does not always execute the will of God as he or she understands it.

This already indicates that the separation of state and religion is not identical to the separation of politics and religion. Religion does not have to remain silent when it comes to politics. It can be a source of inspiration for politicians and it can enhance ethical consciousness and behavior. Therefore, it should not be excluded from politics. It is important to make the distinction between politics and the state. The fact that freedom of religion and the separation of state and religion do not imply the separation of religion and politics can make it easier to impose religious liberty and state neutrality.

Religious people obviously and justifiably fear the separation of religion and politics.

COMMUNITIES AND IDENTITIES LIVING TOGETHER

The religious neutrality of the state does not necessarily lead to religious neutrality of politics. A religion is not allowed to infiltrate the institutions of the state, otherwise it would acquire more power than other religions and therefore destroy religious liberty (a choice for a religion is not free if one religion has more power of persuasion or coercion than another). But a religion is allowed to try to convince a majority, at least as long as it respects human rights, the liberty of other religions and hence the neutrality of the state. The religious majority can then execute the requirements of its religion within these confines. For example, it can take measures to encourage large families, but it cannot impose a certain form of family or discriminate small or single parent families.

The religiously neutral state organizes and legitimizes the coexistence of different autonomous sub-communities each with its own identity, values and norms. It does so by instituting religious freedom and protection for different religions, and by treating all religions equally (and of course by protecting other human rights, enforcing tolerance, etc.). Non-religious sub-communities are also protected in this way. After all, if diversity is possible for religion, why should it not be possible for other kinds of group identity as well? The freedom of religion and the freedom of association are therefore closely linked.

However, it would be erroneous to postulate this neutrality of the state as some kind of absolute principle. Underneath the plurality of individuals and sub-communities there must be a basic overlapping consensus. Human rights such as the freedom of religion must be part of this consensus, a consensus that is not value-neutral because human rights are values and define the difference between right and wrong. These rights have to be general values and norms, overarching the different sub-communities because without them plurality and identity are impossible. Without freedom of religion, there will be religious coercion and some identities will suffer. It is in the interest of the different sub-communities to adopt these general values because communities need diversity for their own protection. It is never clear in advance which groups will suffer from coercion.

The whole is more than the sum of the parts; it is a collective rather than a collection. Diversity manifests itself within an overall or overarching community — a community of communities — that has human rights as its shared values, and state neutrality stops at these human rights. A state should not be neutral as regards human rights. Individuals who represent sub-communities and who violate human rights should be punished because they place themselves outside the general community of diversity, and cannot invoke diversity or human rights — such as the freedom of religion — for their protection. You cannot break a rule and then demand that you can enjoy its protection. It is because of this protection that we see that the rule is often respected, even by people who hold beliefs which are contrary to the rule. This is a fine example of *Realpolitik*.

The general norms regulating and guaranteeing diversity can indeed clash with the particular norms that constitute the (religious) identity of groups or individuals. At first sight, it is not in the interest of Catholicism for instance to accept religious liberty. It would seem to be more in its interest to try to expand the number of Catholics as much as possible and with all possible means. However, if they reject religious liberty and try to convert others with force, then they as well can one day fall victim to religious coercion. It is in their long term interest to accept religious liberty. And in any case, this acceptance only makes certain kinds of expansion impossible, namely forceful expansion. Real expansion of a creed is based on persuasion, and this remains possible in a system of human rights. Even more so: it is *only* possible in such a system.

A more difficult problem is the religious conviction that is contrary to human rights irrespective of efforts to convert others. The values and norms that apply within a sub-community cannot be chosen at random. They have to conform to a certain overarching consensus. They cannot contradict the basic overarching norms of the whole community. If they have an effect on the rights of the members of the sub-community or on the rights of other sub-communities — for example if a norm of a religion requires the death penalty for apostasy or requires forceful conversion — then the religious freedom of this religion must be limited. There has to be as much freedom as possible, and as much consensus as necessary. Sometimes freedom has to be limited. It should not be allowed to violate human rights.

Sub-communities that do not respect this limit cut off the branch they are sitting on. After all, the basic overlapping norms make it possible for different communities with different norms and values to exist and coexist. Groups that violate these norms ultimately endanger their own existence, unless they are large and strong enough to dominate other groups.

A neutral, democratic state that respects human rights governs a community of communities characterized by a minimum number of common basic norms and excludes those who do not respect these norms. A fundamentalist religious group oppressing certain members or using force to convert other groups is prosecuted for violations of human rights, and may lose the protection of the freedom of religion and the freedom of association. Another sub-community, however, that respects human rights even though perhaps the precepts of its religion tell it to do otherwise, knows that it contributes to the protection of the diversity promoting norms of the wider community. Hence, it knows that it protects its own interests as a group with a particular identity, inevitably living in a world of diversity.

Even though some sub-communities may believe that their values and norms are universally valid, they should not try to impose these values and norms on other sub-communities or on the community at large, not only for the sake of human rights, but also for the sake of their own long term existence as separate groups. Only in this way can they counteract a culture of coercion that can one day also be used against them.

The larger community, however, can impose its overarching values and norms on the different sub-communities, because the main function of these overarching values and norms is to facilitate plurality and plurality is only rarely voluntary, especially in matters of religion. Since it is often difficult and undesirable to impose values, the values of the whole should be to a large degree acceptable to the parts, and they are acceptable because they facilitate plurality. The parts can accept them as a guarantee for their own survival, at least to the extent that:

- The parts need plurality and diversity; in other words, they are not strong enough to impose themselves and to suppress other groups, not now and not in the future; and

- The parts have a clear view of what is or is not in their long term interest because they think in a more or less rational way (and not in an emotional way).

INCLUSIVE AND EXCLUSIVE NORMS

It is perhaps useful to make the difference between inclusive and exclusive norms. Contrary to a widely shared opinion, the reason why we have inclusive norms — such as religious liberty, tolerance, and freedom of association — is not to replace or to soften the undesirable consequences of an insufficient sense of common values or community. In fact they are the heart of a community, a community above the different sub-communities, and people can feel just as attached to these inclusive norms, as they feel attached to other, so-called substantive norms or values.

Exclusive norms are norms that do not try to protect plurality or hold together people with different views, but try to win a competitive struggle with other norms. Religious norms are the best examples of such norms. These exclusive norms can threaten the wider community, at least to the extent that they are supposed to be universal and hence imposed on the wider community (or on people who want to leave the group). A sub-community that feels attached to certain exclusive norms or norms that exclude difference — for example, the belief that homosexuals are sinners — may try to impose its norms on the rest of the larger community, even if this means violating human rights, religious freedom and the principle of tolerance. Compared to their own exclusive norms (which are often viewed as divine commandments), human rights and tolerance are, in their eyes, lesser values or of no value at all. In this case, the inclusive norms of the wider community should take precedence over the exclusive norms of the sub-community, whereas normally inclusive norms are there to protect exclusive norms. Some coercion may be necessary as well.

The norms of the larger community should be as inclusive as possible, and should allow for as much plurality as is possible and desirable (plurality of exclusive, inclusive and other norms or practices). Coercion, suppression and judicial action are not the only solutions to the problems posed by certain exclusive norms of sub-communities. Sub-communities should also consider adopting as much inclusive norms as possible. They can value the state as facilitator of plurality, because they benefit from plurality, or they can value human rights because of the universal values which these rights protect.

Of course, this is not always easy. Adopting inclusive norms may require a certain denial of your group-identity for the purpose of protecting your group-identity. Your identity can be based on universal exclusive norms, and therefore on the elimination of difference, but your identity also requires the protection of the state and of the inclusive norms that regulate and protect difference. The state that protects the other groups from the claims of your own group also protects your own group. Other groups may also have exclusive norms and may be stronger than your group, now or in the future.

You can try to use force to change other people's identities into your own universal and exclusive identity — which means that you also have to attack the state, because the state protects difference against you. You might end up destroying the very institutions that protect you against the actions of hostile groups that try to do the same. Alternatively, you do not try this, and you accept certain inclusive norms and the existence of other identities. If you choose the latter option, you are more certain of your survival, but you lose a part of your identity, namely your claim to universality or your principles which violate human rights. However, there may be other ways than force to acquire universality, for example persuasion. Adopting inclusive norms and supporting the state as facilitator of plurality is therefore in everybody's interest, on the condition that everybody or most people adopt these norms and support such a state.

The question is: what do groups consider more important, their own survival, which may imply giving up certain aspects of their identity (or giving up the forceful universal application of certain norms that they feel constitute their identity); or their identity, which implies putting their existence and therefore their identity at risk in a possibly violent struggle with other identities? An identity often requires imposing certain values on the rest of the community, which is likely to be self destructive because other groups can resist or can follow your example.

Again, we all have to share the world with others. Any other mentality will probably cause one's own demise in the long term. This kind of risk promotes the acceptance of inclusive norms such as human rights and religious liberty, and promotes the acceptance of difference. It is, therefore, part of the justification of human rights. It can even justify human rights to people who, a priori, do not sympathize with human rights or who have adopted values and norms that are incompatible with human rights.

Inclusive norms have an exclusive side: one should not be too neutral or too tolerant. Not everything can be included or allowed. Those who attack the inclusive norms are excluded. Everything else should be accepted. The consensus of the community as a whole should be as small as possible and plurality as large as possible, except if the community is united enough to wish otherwise.

Only the attempts to diminish plurality by force and the attempts to attack the system of inclusive norms that protect plurality should be excluded. Exclusive norms as such and peaceful persuasion or voluntary acceptance of exclusive norms, should not be suppressed. The defense of plurality against the imposition of exclusive norms or against attacks on inclusive norms may entail the use of force and a limitation of plurality. We may have to suppress a group — and hence limit plurality — if this group wants to limit plurality.

But other groups and their exclusive norms must be allowed to compete with each other and to strive towards universal acceptance, but only by way of debate protected by human rights and religious liberty, without coercion or forced conversion, and only as long as the identity does not harm the rights of the members. This debate may lead to new universally accepted exclusive or inclusive norms. Some groups may be able to increase their membership and to come a bit closer to universality, but others may not. The fact that human rights make it possible to debate, and that debate makes it possible to achieve universal acceptance of certain exclusive norms, is another reason why groups may decide to accept human rights.

The conflicts caused by the coexistence of different groups — each with their incompatible claims on the other — must be solved by conversation, and not by force. But conversation implies the acceptance of inclusive norms such as human rights. This means that every group identity must contain the acceptance of the importance of human rights, at least regarding the relationships with other groups (groups are allowed to reject human rights for themselves on the condition that they allow people to quit). However, some parts of some groups' identities do not imply this acceptance. As a rule, one should not ask somebody to give up part of his or her identity, except when this identity makes the acceptance of difference impossible and entails the suppression of other identities or the violation of rights of members. In some cases, asking a group to refrain from imposing its identity and its norms and opinions on others means asking the group to give up (part of) its identity, and this is necessary but regrettable (medieval Catholicism would be a hypothetical example of such a group). In other cases, this limitation will not harm the identity of the group (Jews would be an example of such a group because they have no desire to convert others and generally their norms do not violate the rights of members).

The problem of inclusive norms versus exclusive norms often appears in religious matters. Most religions claim to have universal validity. Their values are said to be revealed by God, the only God, and the God of all human beings, the only law-giver, accepting no competition. These values should therefore be the values of all human beings. Those who do not accept these values are sinners, heretics or apostates and must be forcefully converted for their own good. This, together with the fact that values coming from God cannot be contested, makes it imperative that other groups, as well as the state that is the guardian of diversity, disappear. Other religions or atheists are not accepted on an equal basis, and everything contrary to the norms of the religion is something that has to be changed, even if this means changing the lives, habits and convictions of people who do not belong to the religious group in question.

Fundamentalist Muslims or Christians for example try to regulate every aspect of life according to the norms given by their religious belief. This is no problem as long as they limit themselves to their own lives and allow people to leave their group. However, most of the time, they want to regulate other people's lives as well and they prohibit exit attempts (apostasy is a capital crime in Islam). In order to achieve this, they try to take over the state and its instruments of power because that makes their job of exclusion a lot easier. If freedom, diversity and identity mean anything, then we need to stop these people and insulate the state against them. The *reality* of human rights depends on it. However, even these people, when they think rationally as all people can, are able to come to the conclusion that the acceptance of inclusive norms is in their interest and in the general interest of their religion.

CHAPTER 6. THE LAW

THE RULE OF LAW

Perhaps the most important tool we need in order to make rights *real* is the law. Human rights must be translated in laws, laws moreover that are enforced, that are the highest laws of the nation, and that cannot be overruled by other laws. If our rights are violated, then a judge and a police force must be able to enforce respect for the law. This implies the rule of law. The rule of law makes rights *real* in two ways: it ensures the enforcement of human rights and it creates a limited state and hence a free society in which people can use their rights unhindered by the state.

The rule of law means that the state is bound by law and is therefore a limited state. It is bound to respect the laws, inter alia the laws protecting human rights. It cannot do anything it wants, it can only do what a law permits or forces it to do. A limited state is not necessarily a weak state, although that is a reproach often directed at states bound by the rule of law. A limited state can be very strong, vigorous and effective within the imposed boundaries of power, even more so than a state that tries to do everything. In addition, when a state is limited in its actions by the law that says what it should and should not do, a free society independent of power is created. State and society become different spheres and in the latter sphere an independent and free social life can start to blossom, undisturbed by state interference and coercion. Because abuse of power by states is a traditional cause of human rights violations, the *reality* of human rights depends on this free space, and hence depends on the rule of law and the resulting separation of state and society.

The state is not allowed to determine all human actions. It can interfere only in a specific number of domains, namely those domains that are regulated by the law. One and perhaps the most important of these domains is the protection of human rights. The range, the power of penetration and the competence of the state are limited and meet with a society that is to a certain extent impenetrable for the state; "to a certain extent" because not everything is allowed in society, and sometimes the state has to interfere, otherwise it would have no "raison d'être". Let us not forget that human rights can be violated by citizens in civil society. However, society, as far as it respects human rights, is more than an object of political interference. It is also a space of freedom, undisturbed by the state and in which there is a plurality of free and autonomous individuals and groups, each with their own identity and rules. These individuals and groups can be mutually incompatible and can clash and contradict each other, as long as the laws that regulate these clashes (e.g. human rights laws) are respected.

The rule of law — the principle that the state can only do what the law allows it to do — is not a sufficient condition for a *real* protection of human rights. The law can permit or even compel to violate rights, and it can be written in such a vague and general way that the limits on state actions are close to nothing. Laws can allow the state to interfere drastically in the lives of individuals or in the affairs of groups in civil society. Many tyrannies have laws and even use laws to oppress people, to destroy the free space of society, and to violate rights.

That is why the rule of law cannot possibly mean that everything can be written into a law. If that were the case, then the rule of law would be a meaningless concept. The rule of law is in fact shorthand for the rule of a special kind of law, namely the rule of the law which translates and protects human rights. Even in a democratic rule of law, where the law originates from the will of the people, are there limits on what the law can be. A law can never contradict human rights because the purpose of law is precisely the protection of human rights. Popular sovereignty is limited by human rights.

A complete description of the rule of law would also contain other elements. The definition of the law in the rule of law is not limited to the compatibility of the law and human rights. The law must also be stable and predictable in order to avoid that every arbitrary act of state takes on the cloak of the law and thereby seeks the protection of the law. Moreover, only predictable laws can be respected. And respect for the law is part of the rule of law.

On top of that, laws must not be too numerous, otherwise it is again very difficult to respect the law. A large number of laws is also incompatible with one of the goals of the rule of law, namely the creation of a space of freedom. The more laws, the smaller this space of freedom (although one very general and vague law can also reduce this space to nothing).

Only if these three conditions — a definition of the law that excludes laws that contradict human rights, and predictable laws that are relatively few in number — are met, can there be a real rule of law, a limited state and a relatively free civil society. All this is linked to human rights because there are certain human rights that specifically install and protect the rule of law. But there is a two-way causation at work here, as so often in the system of human rights. In one direction, human rights install the rule of law and therefore create a limited state and a free society. They make it impossible for the state to hold individuals or groups responsible for no matter what action they undertake (some rights directly institutionalize the rule of law and human rights in general limit the content of laws and hence create a free space). Responsibility, conviction, punishment, etc. cannot cover everything, only those things translated into stable and predictable laws that conform to human rights. As a result, there exists a relatively large domain outside of the reach of the state and the law, a domain in which individuals and groups can unfold their own autonomous, self chosen private or public activities and thoughts, free from political leadership, control or interference.

In the other direction, there is also a causal link. Institutionalizing human rights institutionalizes the rule of law and the separation between state and society, but the opposite is also true. The rule of law and the separation of state and society promote human rights, even though there are states that apply the rule of law and that have a relatively free civil society, but that fail to enforce and respect all or some human rights. A limited state has less opportunity and power to violate human rights than a state that is not limited.

The same is true for a state that has to deal with the criticism of a free society. Furthermore, in a free society groups of different kinds can be vehicles for the promotion of human rights.

Human rights institutionalize the rule of law, and the rule of law can make human rights *real*, but the rule of law can exist without human rights (many things other than human rights can limit government action and can determine laws, for example divine commandments). However, without human rights, we are clearly dealing with another kind of rule of law.

A few final additional remarks: no matter how important the rule of law, we should avoid turning the rule of law into a dictatorship of the law. The question "what is a good law?" must always remain open. The law, even though it rules, has to be actively criticized, otherwise we get a fetishism of the law, an unconditional surrender to the law, whatever its content and meaning. Then we end up with positivism, as described in Chapter 1. The necessary permanence of the law — permanence is necessary because of predictability and therefore respect — should not become a dogma either, because in that case the question of the good law will likewise disappear.

One other characteristic of the law should not be overlooked. The law must be blind when it comes to individuals and individual interests. This is the origin of the famous image of Justice as a blindfolded woman. The law cannot give advantages or punishments to some individuals only. It has to be general and neutral regarding individuals. It has to be applicable to everyone in the same way, or to no one. It cannot be for or against certain persons. The law is equal for everybody, and everybody is equal before the law. Only then can justice be served and can the rule of law exist. In any other case will the law be an instrument in the rule of some over others. An related advantage is that the likelihood of oppressive laws becomes smaller. If those who make the laws are subject to the laws just like anyone else, then they will think twice before voting an oppressive law.

The limits on the content of the law, imposed by the rule of law, guarantee that no legislator can demand that his or her will becomes the law, whatever it is and without further conditions. The people as well do not have absolute popular sovereignty. They cannot use the law to harm the rights of the minority. A democracy is more than just the rule of the majority. There is no *real* democracy without the rule of law as it is described here. After all, a tyranny can also have the consent of a majority, so a democracy is more than a system of majority rule.

A democratic law is a limited law. Even in a perfect democracy, it is possible to limit the will of the people. The people or the majority of the people cannot exercise their power in an unlimited way, otherwise we would not have democracy but the tyranny of the majority. If my rights are violated by a tyrant or by the majority, it does not make a lot of difference. The majority can decide and can impose its will on the minority, but this does not mean that the minority has to accept everything, including rights violations. A minority is not entirely powerless in a democracy. Thanks to the rule of law, it can use its rights and the laws that protect these rights in order to defend itself against certain decisions of the majority. It can use the rule of law against the rule of the majority.

STATE AND SOCIETY

The border between the state and society, instituted by the rule of law, is not always what it seems or what it is considered to be. The fact that the state is not omnipresent, is no "Panopticon", and cannot spread itself uniformly over the whole of society, does not mean that the state stops where society starts. The state can legitimately interfere in society. The border is not an iron curtain. If civil society would be sovereign in its own house, anarchy and lawlessness would be the consequence and there would be no reason to have a state in the first place. There is interference in society, but inside society there is also a space that the law cannot appropriate and in which man is free, on the condition that his free actions do not contradict the law or are not a subject of legitimate legislation (that is, legislation that is not contrary to human rights, that springs from the will of the people and that maintains the rule of law). Where the law is silent, man can do as he likes. So society is split up between areas of freedom and areas of legitimate interference.

Another misunderstanding is that the border between state and society corresponds to the border between public and private. It does not because private as well as public things happen in civil society, and political things happen in society. Especially in a democracy do we see that political life takes place in both the state and society. Democracy would be impossible without this and cannot accommodate an equation between society and privacy. It is equally wrong to equate the public domain with the domain of the law, and the private domain with the domain of freedom. The private sphere is subject to the rule of law, as much as the public sphere, and the latter is as much a domain of freedom as the former. Freedom and the law are not a straightforward translation of private and public respectively.

Democracy proves that "politics" and "state" are not absolutely the same thing. Without making the difference between these two words it is impossible to hold on to the difference between state and society. Democracy requires the elimination of the difference between rulers and ruled. Democratic politics is everybody's business and takes place, to a large extent, in society. When the citizens and the state desperately try to avoid each other as much as possible — as is implicit in the doctrine of the separation of state and society — then politics becomes a matter only for politicians, and political life becomes something alien, a necessary evil perhaps or a mechanism for coercion instead of a source of values. For clarity's sake, I have tried to put all these things in a drawing:

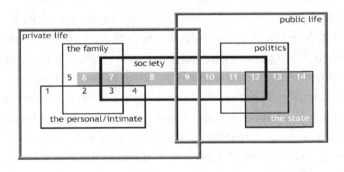

Some examples of the meaning of the digits:

1: Loneliness, philosophical convictions.

2: Unspoken marital hatred, marital fidelity, adultery; the latter may, in countries where adultery is illegal, belong to the gray area — this gray area is the scope of legislation.

3: Certain moral convictions about family life; the reason for the link with society is that these convictions are often influenced by society.

4: Political, moral and other convictions unrelated to the family.

The common characteristic of points 1 to 4 is that they deal with thoughts and convictions and are therefore outside of the scope of legislation.

5: The division of labor in the family.

6: Violence within the family.

7: Raising children in the family, but not the specific task of educating children in the family, because education, contrary to raising children in general, is a public activity. Education is the transmission of public knowledge and must be classified under 9. It can and does happen in the family as well as in school, but I did not make the drawing detailed enough to incorporate it (that would have resulted in an unintelligible drawing).

8: A sports club.

9: A school, a church.

10: A cultural society.

11: Political participation outside government institutions, political demonstrations, pressure groups, lobbying (political convictions, mentioned above at number 4, should perhaps be classified under this number, but this also would make the drawing unintelligible; in any case, reality is too complicated to be forced into a simple drawing).

12: Political participation within government institutions, village meetings, civil disobedience, a court of justice with a jury-system, political parties.

13: Representative politics, parliament, a court of justice without a jury-system, espionage (espionage is obviously not a public activity, but it is nevertheless part of public life because in a democracy, espionage must become public after the fact; it is a secret activity, not because it should never be known to the public, but because it involves acts that temporarily require secrecy in order to be successful and effective but that can be declassified after some time).

14: Government administration, government bureaucracy.

Both the public and the private spaces are at the same time spaces of freedom (in the limited sense of freedom from state interference) and spaces subject to the provisions of the law. The latter are shown as gray areas. As stated above, all state activity is regulated by the law, while the part of the private sphere which corresponds to the purely individual or personal is entirely free from government interference, or better should be. Needless to say that the drawing depicts an ideal situation.

Civil society is created by the principle of the separation of state and society. This principle makes society to a certain extent independent from power and the state, but it is itself dependent on another principle, namely the rule of law, which in turn depends on human rights. But, conversely, effective protection of human rights requires both the rule of law and the freedom of society.

Chapter 7. Separation of Powers and Judicial Review

Protection by the Courts

The rule of law, and hence the *reality* of human rights translated into laws, requires the enforcement of the law. The responsibility of the legislator — to vote for laws that protect human rights, and to avoid voting for laws that reduce human rights — is supplemented by the responsibility of the courts and the police force to uphold and enforce the rule of law (the responsibility of the police force being added to the responsibility of the courts). A good law, i.e. a law that respects human rights, that is predictable, etc., is insufficient. The courts have to monitor respect for the law and punish rights violations or actions that contradict the laws that protect human rights. They punish actions by both citizens and governments, which is why the executive branch of power and the judiciary have to be separate institutions. Without such separate institutions, a government cannot correct itself.

Law enforcement is one way to protect human rights. But courts also act in a more indirect way. They react not only to actions that violate human rights but also to laws that do the same. There is no guarantee, after all, that the legislator always acts responsibly or never makes mistakes. The law can be used to oppress. Even a democratic majority is not always right or righteous.

Some types of courts in particular, such as the US Supreme Court, monitor legislation. This is a second way in which courts enforce human rights, and this is also an instance of law enforcement, even if it means repealing laws, because the courts enforce the higher law at the expense of the lower one. They verify that laws do not contradict the constitution and the rights protected by it. The necessity to verify and possibly repeal laws that violate human rights or the constitution is the reason why the legislative branch of power and the judiciary have to be separated. In a short space of time, we have seen two examples of how a separation of powers is necessary for a *real* protection of human rights.

Verifying the compatibility of laws and the constitution is called judicial review. Judicial review can result in the judicial verdict that a particular law is "null and void". This law can then no longer be applied and rights will be protected by this non-application. Every citizen can address a review request to the court if he or she thinks that a law violates certain rights enshrined in the constitution.[1] The court then enforces the rule that the legislator does not have absolute freedom. Human rights, at least to the extent that they are protected by the constitution, can be used against the legislator. The "tyranny of the majority" (or of any other legislator) is made impossible and we are reminded that a democracy is much more than simple majority rule. Protection of human rights is just as much part of democracy, if only because democracy cannot function without these rights (see Chapter 9). And the reality of these rights requires judicial review and separation of powers. If laws can be anything, if the legislator has the last word and if there is no way to invalidate laws that contradict the rights of the constitution, then these rights are worth no more than the paper they are written on.

Judicial review is not a limitation of democracy, and is not a just or unjust constraint on the power of the people and their representatives. Neither is it part of some struggle for power between the judiciary and the legislature, or between "activist judges" and the majority of the people. The constitution, against which laws are tested, is also a product of the legislature and is, in the ideal case, subject to democratic approval (the people should be able to vote on the constitution). A Supreme Court of some kind only verifies whether

---

1 In some countries, courts also have the right to review compatibility between laws and international treaties. Like a constitution, treaties are a kind of higher law, and normal municipal laws should not contradict the higher laws.

the inferior law conforms to the superior one. It does not legislate, not even in a negative way, by invalidating laws, and so it does not usurp democratic or legislative rights. It only ensures that the inferior legislator — parliament — respects the rules decided by the superior legislator — the constitutional assembly and the people.

There is no reason to call judicial review an interference of non-elected judges in politics, a criticism often directed against the US Supreme Court. Judges merely apply the law, and in doing so limit the range of the legislature. The whole idea behind the doctrine of the separation of powers is not separation but limitation, checks and balances. Why should parliament be a supreme power with absolute freedom of action? Judges have a veto-power, but not the last word. The people keep the last word, but then they may have to change the constitution, and the procedures to change the constitution are such that they force the people to reflect very carefully before taking that road. Without a difference between a relatively fixed constitution containing basic principles, and regular laws that are easy to change, the risks of losing these basic principles is too high. If human rights protection is organized by normal laws, then it can be undone by normal laws, voted by a simple majority in a parliament that can have a completely different composition after the next election. Rights are not completely safe in the constitution either, because this can also be changed, but nothing is ever completely safe. And without a difference between a constitution and a normal law, judges would be unable to limit the content of normal laws to those rules that are compatible with higher principles.

It is true that judicial review favors conservatism because the judges can undo efforts towards change but cannot change anything themselves.[2] But what they try to conserve is of the utmost importance and hence conservatism is the right policy in this case. A conservative judicial "expertocracy" is to be feared when it consists of non-elected, undemocratic and unaccount-

---

2 This is not entirely true in the Anglo-Saxon law tradition, in which a judge does not simply execute and apply the law (the judge being "the mouth of the law") but can also create new law by developing existing law. He or she can go from specific rules to more general ones, or can take decisions in previous and similar cases into account for the sake of judicial consistency. A decision of a judge does not only influence the case at hand. It can become a judicial precedent and have consequences for future cases. Strictly speaking, a judicial verdict only binds the parties to the case. But if an authoritative institution issues a verdict, then it will have an effect on future cases. The advantage is continuity and predictability. People who wonder whether their actions are legal or not can look at judicial verdicts and adapt their actions if necessary.

able individuals who take their decisions outside of the public debate, and who may have the intention of voting laws that violate the rights contained in the constitution. If that is the purpose, then it is better to change the constitution or to start a revolution.

As long as you choose to remain in the existing system, you have to accept that the system operates and that someone enforces coherence in the system of law and invalidates laws that are incompatible with higher laws. Without judicial review, there is no way to enforce this coherence. Not only would rights suffer, because there would be no way to invalidate laws that violate rights, but the entire system as such would break down because of internal contradictions.

If rights are to be *real*, then we need good laws that translate rights and other laws that do not harm rights. But we also need courts to enforce the laws and the police to enforce the verdicts of the courts. And, finally, we need a separation of powers because:

- •Law enforcement may be at the expense of some parts of the government, and

- •Courts should not only limit the actions of other government powers but also the laws that these powers wish to impose.

Declarations of rights, or even the translation of rights into laws, are clearly not enough. Monitoring observance of the law and, if necessary, enforcement of the law are also necessary. And enforcement requires separation of powers. Without this separation, an individual citizen is unable to protect his or her rights against a powerful government. He or she must have the possibility of using one part of government against another part, either because the actions of this other part violate his or her rights, or because this part imposes laws that ultimately will violate rights or at least fail to protect rights sufficiently. If powers are not separated, then the individual stands before a uniform block of power, without defense. It may even happen that powers collaborate in order to violate his or her rights. In some parts of the world, it is not uncommon that judges punish individuals at the request of the government and that the police executes this punishment at the same request. Power protects against power, and government against government.

Judicial review is not an easy business. Some laws do not violate but limit rights. For example, they exclude the use of rights in a way that is in fact an abuse of rights (e.g. the use of rights as a means to harm the rights of others; see Chapter 3). Judicial review is therefore limited. Laws that legitimately limit rights provision of the constitution cannot be invalidated because of unconstitutionality. The rights provisions of most constitutions provide the possibility that they are limited in the case of abuse.

Judges who engage in judicial review have to make some fine distinctions between illegitimate violations of rights and legitimate limits on rights. They have to judge whether a law justifiably limits human rights, or limits rights for the wrong reasons or excessively, and hence violates them. Is the law that limits rights a necessary measure or could some other, less far-reaching solution have been found in order to solve the perceived problem? Are the limits imposed on rights by the law in proportion to the good that the law wishes to achieve? Not an easy job for anyone to answer these questions.

For example, in a country without a well-functioning education system but with an important and active anti-democratic movement, it may be necessary to legislate and impose limits on the freedom of expression. In another country, it may be better not to impose such limits and try to eradicate anti-democrats by way of education and the passing of time.

Separation of powers means limitations on powers. The power of the legislature, and hence of the people, is limited in several ways. In the previous chapter, we have seen that a law cannot be anything. There are certain limits on the content of a law. Hence, the legislator cannot legislate everything he or she wants. For example, laws cannot contradict human rights. The law is more than the will of the people. It has to respect certain rules independently of the will of anybody.[3] Secondly, a legislator who does not respect these limits faces another power that will enforce these limits. The legislature has to respect this power. And, finally, the separation of power within the legislature, between two chambers, limits the actions of each chamber. Mistakes by one chamber, or a lack of forethought, can be corrected by the other chamber.

---

3 The fact that laws cannot contradict human rights is only one rule; others are that there cannot be "ex post facto" laws, that there must be some continuity, predictability, clarity and coherence,, etc.

The right to appeal is also a separation of powers, within the judiciary this time, again with the purpose of correcting mistakes or prejudices by one court. This is necessary because a verdict of a judge can imply a violation of human rights. Just as one cannot be sure that the legislator acts responsibly, one cannot be sure of a judge. But if two or more judges decide against you in the same way, then it becomes difficult to argue incompetence, irresponsibility, malignancy or prejudice.

If citizens violate human rights, then the victims can call on the state to act. If the state violates human rights, either in its actions or laws, then the citizens can use one part of the state against another. However, what if both the legislature and the judiciary are dysfunctional or outright irresponsible? What if the law is a bad law and the judges fail to invalidate it, because of incompetence, under-funding or perhaps even connivance with the legislature? Or what if the law is OK but is not enforced by the courts? International law, international law enforcement or intervention can perhaps help to make rights *real* (see Chapter 10), but states still have means to repel international intervention. Civil disobedience or, in structural cases, revolution then seem to be the only options left in the struggle for the *reality* of rights.

CIVIL DISOBEDIENCE

Regarding civil disobedience, you have to be careful when allowing yourself to defy the law. Civil disobedience is not the same thing as the freedom of conscience. You do have the absolute legal right to believe what you want and what your conscience forces you to believe. But it is another thing to be able to act according to your conscience, or not to act because of your conscience, as is often the case with conscientious objectors. If you state that everything, even a breach of the law, is allowed as long as it conforms to your conscience, then you go down a very dangerous path.

The freedom of conscience is something different from the right to do or not to do something because of objections based on conscience. You may be forced to do something that goes against your conscience while retaining your freedom of conscience and your beliefs about wrong and right. You can even force yourself to act against your conscience, perhaps because of a sense of duty or because of respect for the rule of law. You only lose your freedom of conscience when you are forced to believe something, which can only happen in extreme circumstances.

Conscience as the ability to know wrong from right is a kind of self legislation. But because this is fallible (in German they say, "das Gewissen ist kein Wissen", conscience is not knowledge), and more fallible than common legislation (more fallible because you are alone — two people know more than one — and because you miss the opportunity to learn from discussion and arguments), it should not determine actions when it is incompatible with the laws that are valid in a well-functioning democracy. Only if the external law, as opposed to the internal law, is clearly dysfunctional, can there be a reason to appeal to your conscience and engage in civil disobedience.

However, civil disobedience is an individual choice, and can it be allowed that individuals decide for themselves whether a system of law is "clearly dysfunctional"? It is dangerous at least, which is why civil disobedience should be an emergency measure only. The risk of anarchy can sometimes convince us to accept a supposedly dysfunctional law or judge, even if our conscience tells us to rebel.

The Justice System

Courts must protect human rights and rights cannot become *real* without them, but it is common that courts are used against human rights, either by the executive or by some party in a court procedure. That is why there are rules for the functioning of courts.

Court procedures and verdicts must be public. Justice must not only be done, it must also be seen to be done. Publicity is in the interest of justice, justice in the sense of an effective court working to realize human rights or to punish violations. Every trial is a "show trial". The publicity of a trial makes it possible to judge the judge and to decide whether he or she has adequately defended human rights. The secret trial is typical of authoritarian regimes because it allows for abuses of power. It is very hard to use a public trial for power games or oppression. But even when there is no dictator wishing to use the courts for his power play, there is a risk of injustice. False accusations or false testimonies are more likely to remain undiscovered in a closed trial. It is not only the state that can gain from a closed trial.

However, publicity alone does not guarantee that trials and verdicts are fair and just (which is shown by the phenomenon of communist show trials). Just as important is the rule that the judge is impartial, and above all impartial with regard to the executive who is often tempted to see the justice system as its strong arm.

If a court is to respect the human rights of a defendant, then the following rules apply. The defendant should have the possibility to defend himself or have himself defended. That is, after all, why he is called a "defendant". If necessary, he should receive free legal assistance. He must be able to argue his case and to give counter-arguments, to call witnesses for the defense and to question witnesses for the prosecution. He should not be forced to confess or to incriminate himself (the right to remain silent). He is innocent until proven guilty. And if proven guilty, he should not suffer excessively tough penalties that would limit his human rights disproportionately, and he should have the possibility to appeal to a higher court (a second chance to undo mistakes made by the lower court). All the safeguards mentioned here do not exclude miscarriages of justice. These are possible in the best systems.

Before the court proceedings start, the defendant should be swiftly indicted of a crime and informed on the nature of the indictment. He should not be held in detention without such an indictment. The time he spends in detention between the moment of indictment and the moment of the verdict, should not be excessively long. After a not-guilty verdict resulting from a fair trial, he should be released immediately and should not be subjected to a new trial for the same offence ("ne bis in idem", no two trials for the same offense).

"Nulla poena sine lege": no crime or punishment without a law voted and published before the criminal deed. In other words, no retroactive laws, no laws with retroactive effect or "ex post facto" laws (laws that make deeds punishable after they have been committed). One cannot punish people for acts that were not a crime at the time when they were committed because people should know what is or is not allowed and should be able to plan their actions in the manner of a law-abiding citizen. Laws should therefore be public as well, for the same reason.

Again for the same reason, laws should be predictable and should not change all the time. Nobody is responsible for a violation of a law if the law changes from day to day, because if the law changes constantly, then nobody knows the law and nobody can respect the law. Predictability and permanence of the law are prerequisites for obedience, just as knowledge and publicity.

There should not be too many rules, otherwise people will find it hard to respect them all and will violate them inadvertently. The judges and the police will not have enough time to enforce them all or to punish all violations of all rules, which leads to injustice.

All these elements put together make the justice system just, and protect the citizens against the state or against fellow citizens that want to abuse the justice system and include it in some plan to violate rights. These rules also protect citizens against inadvertent violations of rights that may result from dysfunctional judicial proceedings. These rules do not guarantee but at least promote the use of the justice system for the goal it is supposed to serve, namely the protection and *realization* of human rights. If one element is missing, then all the others may become useless. Most of them are included in the main human rights instruments.

Chapter 8. Tolerance

No Human Rights Without Tolerance

Human rights have no meaning or *reality* without tolerance. Tolerance is a necessary consequence of human rights. Human rights create difference and plurality, and tolerance is needed to accept this plurality and to accept human rights as the causes of this plurality. It is useless to have the right to express an opinion freely if afterwards this expression is not tolerated. Tolerance is respect for the other point of view that is expressed with the help of human rights. Respect not necessarily in the sense of accepting the content of the other point of view (because then there would not be a need for tolerance), nor of admiring the content of the other point of view — in the way we might respect a writer, without automatically accepting everything he or she says. This kind of respect is easy.

The problem, and the need for tolerance and respect, concerns those expressions or practices which we do not admire, which we disagree with or which perhaps we loathe. We have to respect and accept, not the truth or value of these expressions and practices — that might be impossible — but their existence. We feel that another opinion or habit has the right to exist, but at the same time we disagree with it, and we might even loathe it. Respect in this sense does not mean that we have to avoid contradicting other people or arguing against them.

Again, as for example in the case of economic rights and freedom rights, there is a reverse causation at work: tolerance supports human rights and can make them *real*, but human rights also support tolerance and can make it real. Freedom of expression can be used to enforce tolerance, but this freedom also puts us in a position that allows us to learn and study other opinions. Hence, we have a better chance of understanding these other opinions and their causes in reasoning, education, etc. And a better understanding promotes tolerance.

If human rights require the support of tolerance, then human rights require a certain mentality, a certain attitude of respect towards other people. Respect for other points of view or other practices means respect for other people and for the fact that they are different. Opinion and identity are to a large extent the same thing. Accepting people as they are, as they think and do, is an attitude and a mentality required by human rights. It is no use accepting human rights if you do not accept this. One could even say that people have a right to respect and tolerance. This right is a logical consequence of all other human rights. People have this right because they have human rights and because they use these rights to manifest themselves in different ways.

However, tolerance means more than passive respect, more than leaving everybody to their own devices. It means more than letting people do their own thing and it is more than a lack of interest or concern. Sometimes it may require active protection of somebody's difference, and punishment of those who fail to show respect. Passive tolerance must be combined with active protection against intolerance and against the imposition of a point of view, an identity or a way of life. Respect is not enough. When you respect your fellow man without responsibility, you are certain to leave him alone when it would be better to intervene, to help or to punish. Tolerance should not imply egoism or egocentrism.

THE BENEFITS OF TOLERANCE

This shows that we have to be careful with words like "tolerance" and "respect". Another person, another opinion or another way of life is not just something we have to tolerate like we tolerate bad weather. Social life is not completely negative or meaningless. The company of other people is not only a burden we have to tolerate, and it certainly is more than a matter of indifference (in the sense of making no difference) or lack of interest. The company of others is beneficial and necessary for the realization of some of the most important human values. The other person is a necessary part of each human life. We not only tolerate the other person, we also use him, follow him, contradict him, discuss with him, help him, etc.

Diversity and tolerance of diversity can be very beneficial because they make it possible for us to learn from others, to see how things look from a completely different point of view, to debate with others and to take into account their objections and counter-arguments. Tolerance will therefore help us to come closer to the truth. We can take advantage of diversity and of tolerance of diversity, because diversity means other opinions and criticism of our own opinions. The school of tolerance teaches people to reap the benefits from conflict and difference,[1] and makes people suspicious of all efforts to eliminate conflict or to let it degenerate into violence. Tolerance is more than just a restraint on violence. It contributes in a positive way to diversity and hence to the benefits of diversity.

This already indicates that diversity is not something static. Tolerance does not mean accepting diversity as it is and as it will always be. The purpose of tolerance is not to make opinions coexist without interaction of any kind other than bare acceptance or indifference, and acceptance is more than an armistice necessary to keep the peace between interests of which no single one is strong enough to impose itself. It must be possible to convince other people. The function of tolerance is not to separate opinions, nor to maintain differences as they are. Its function is to make confrontation between opinions possible. Tolerance merely separates aggressive people. It does not keep people as such, let alone points of view, out of each other's way. Confrontation can, of course, modify points of view and can eliminate (or enhance) differences. We have opinions on opinions, we judge, we convince, we become convinced, and we change our opinions accordingly. That is why difference in a tolerant world is something dynamic.

This also implies that it is not because we tolerate someone or some point of view, that we do not have the right to say that this person is mistaken or the right to try to convince this person. Without the possibility to convince, the right to free expression loses much of its meaning. The pleasure of ex-

---

1 Little, D. 1996, "Tolerance, Equal Freedom, and Peace", in *United States Institute for Peace*, passim.

pressing an opinion is not then main reason for expressing it. In most cases, we express an opinion because we want to convince other people.

Given the importance of convincing, we should not blame people for being intolerant when they criticize another point of view. You can be tolerant and "politically incorrect" at the same time. After all, tolerance is there to make criticism possible. Without tolerance, there is no space for criticism and only a world where people force each other. You are intolerant only when you suppress opinions or customs, when you persecute, physically attack or discriminate people who have another opinion or custom, or when you use force to change people's opinions or customs.

Tolerant people therefore do not have to leave things as they are — for the love of peace, because of indifference, lack of power, or whatever. If you want things to be different, go ahead and argue. You should not be accused of intolerance. Tolerance is sterile when it is no more than putting up with each other or simply being kind enough not to persecute people with other beliefs. Tolerance should be a tool to create relationships and spaces of criticism and persuasion. Only then can it be a productive tolerance, allowing us to reap the benefits of difference.

However, taking into account the importance of convincing could lead to another aberration. Tolerance should not be considered as something temporary, necessary as long as opinions differ. Opinions will most probably always differ, and we will therefore always need tolerance.

TOLERATING INTOLERANCE?

The fact that tolerance is linked to persuasion and that persuasion implies a difference between good and bad opinions already indicates that tolerance is not the same thing as relativism, a-moralism, nihilism or agnosticism. Tolerance does not mean that everything is equally good and valuable or equally deserving. It makes it possible for people to argue the value of their point of view or lifestyle.

There is still another reason why tolerance cannot imply absolute relativism. Tolerance should not be self destructive and therefore should not extend to what is harmful for it. The enemies of tolerance — and therefore the enemies of human rights since there is a link between tolerance and rights — cannot claim to be tolerated. If they are tolerated, then they will, of course, destroy tolerance as well as the institutions that protect tolerance (such as human rights). Unlimited tolerance — tolerance even of intolerance — destroys itself, or at least helps those who want to destroy it. A tolerant society disappears if it tolerates certain things for too long. Intolerant people can use tolerance and the institutions of tolerance in order to destroy tolerance. It is unreasonable to demand that a system — in this case a tolerant system — contains the seeds of its own destruction. One cannot reasonably impose fatal contradictions upon a system, so one cannot impose tolerance for intolerance.

We can and should therefore make a difference between what is good and bad for tolerance, and also between what is good and bad for human rights (because of the link between human rights and tolerance). In any case, it is difficult to see how intolerant people can honestly complain if they are not tolerated.

> [O]ne has no title to object to the conduct of others that is in accordance with principles one would use in similar circumstances to justify one's actions towards them. A person's right to complain is limited to violations of principles he acknowledges himself.[2]

You should not ask something for yourself — i.e., tolerance — that you deny to others. Tolerance and respect must therefore be limited. Not everything should be tolerated. Those who are intolerant or who want to destroy the institutions that protect tolerance — maybe for reasons other than their intolerance — should not be tolerated and should be attacked with their own weapons of intolerance. Their freedom and rights are limited, at least if they put their ideas into practice and cause violations of other people's rights.

Only tolerance and, at most, theoretical intolerance can be tolerated. Tolerating violations of human rights is a logical contradiction, because human rights guarantee tolerance and because tolerance guarantees human rights. If you want to enjoy the benefits of tolerance — for example as a means to protect your own opinions — then you have to respect human rights. Tolerance and human rights go together. You cannot choose one without the other. You cannot violate human rights and expect to be tolerated, no more than you can claim rights and reject tolerance. Rights without tolerance are nonsense, because tolerance protects the use of rights.

---

2 Rawls, J. 1999, *A Theory of Justice*, Oxford: Oxford University Press, p. 190.

Limiting the things that can be tolerated and limiting the rights of the intolerant is only one way to stop them. Paradoxically, we can also stop them by protecting their rights.

> The liberties of the intolerant may persuade them to a belief in freedom. This persuasion works on the psychological principle that those whose liberties are protected by and who benefit from a just constitution will, other things equal, acquire an allegiance to it over a period of time.[3]

Of course, the intolerant can be so fanatical or their power may grow so rapidly that this strategy is unsuccessful or naive. More forceful measures against intolerance are then necessary.

The risk of equating tolerance with relativism, agnosticism, nihilism or skepticism is that people will start to doubt the superior value of human rights. This will endanger the institutions that protect tolerance and will ultimately endanger tolerance itself. A relativistic type of tolerance is therefore self destructive. If all opinions are equally valid, then also opinions on human rights and tolerance. Only if people believe strongly in human rights will tolerance be safe. Skepticism and doubt are incompatible with such a strong belief. They are paralyzing and they leave the field to those who want to destroy human rights.

If tolerance needs human rights, then it cannot be equated with skepticism and doubt. Tolerance needs a strong belief and an active involvement in human rights. It needs a kind of certainty or conviction instead of passive doubt. Anti-rights fanatics will not stop to doubt and will take our passivity as an invitation to act. If we want to defend ourselves, we also have to be fanatical, fanatical rights-activists. Those who tolerate everything will be overrun.

> [A]gnosticism is not a particularly useful defense against fanaticism, and tolerant skeptics who think that nothing can be known are ineffectual allies of civilization when zealots who think they know everything are on the march. ... Tolerance is a beneficent and admirable posture, but in itself it can stop nothing. It refrains from doing harm but may permit harm to be done. ... The struggle for liberty requires an energized faith. ... [I]n a world of necessary actions and ineluctable consequences ... , the liberal's diffidence cannot mean that nothing happens, only that he causes nothing to happen. He may modestly abstain from acting on behalf of public goods that he does not think can be legitimated, but his reticence only means that private and clearly illegitimate forces will control his destiny unopposed. ... Uproot principle, deny the possibility of mutual knowledge of public goods, and what is left except bigotry and brute force?[4]

---

3 Ibidem, p. 192.
4 Barber, op. cit., p. 105-6.

Tolerance in the guise of skepticism and relativism clears the way for tyranny and intolerance because it leads to doubt, paralysis and powerlessness in the face of anti-rights fanatics waiting at the border or organizing within the community. Fanaticism should not always be a dirty word. It is a necessary addition to tolerance and the only way to protect tolerance.

> Relativism — the doctrine that maintains that all values are merely relative and which attacks all 'privileged perspectives' — must ultimately end up undermining democratic and tolerant values as well. Relativism is not a weapon that can be aimed selectively at the enemies one chooses. It fires indiscriminately, shooting out the legs of not only the 'absolutisms', dogmas, and certainties of the Western tradition, but that tradition's emphasis on tolerance, diversity, and freedom of thought as well. If nothing can be true absolutely, if all values are culturally determined, then cherished principles like human equality have to go by the wayside as well.[5]

It is evident that a tolerant system cannot be viewed as one that imposes nothing in terms of values. It imposes human rights because there is no tolerance without them. Not all values are equally valuable. Rights proponents must stick to their opinions and at the same time accept that other people do the same thing, but only as long as these other people — who may be intolerant or opposed to rights — do not actively try to impose their values. Tolerance is not indulgence towards those who are wrong. We cannot allow intolerant or anti-rights people to do what they want. No system, and certainly not a system of tolerance, can be required to contain the seeds of its own destruction or to remain passive in the face of attack.

---

5 Fukuyama, F. 1992, *The End of History and the Last Man*, Harmondsworth: Penguin Books, p. 332.

Chapter 9. Democracy

Political Rights

Democracy is a human right and is as such included in a number of the most important international human rights standards, such as the Universal Declaration of Human Rights, article 21:

> Everyone has the right to take part in the government of his country, directly or through freely chosen representatives. . . . The will of the people shall be the basis of the authority of government; this will shall be expressed in periodic and genuine elections which shall be by universal and equal suffrage and shall be held by secret vote or by equivalent free voting procedures.

See also article 25 of the International Covenant on Civil and Political Rights:

> Every citizen shall have the right and the opportunity, without . . . unreasonable restrictions: (a) To take part in the conduct of public affairs, directly or through freely chosen representatives; (b) To vote and to be elected at genuine periodic elections which shall be by universal and equal suffrage and shall be held by secret ballot, guaranteeing the free expression of the will of the electors.

These are the so-called political rights that together constitute the right to democracy. The existence of this right to democracy was once again confirmed by a vote in the UN Commission on Human Rights in Geneva in

1999 (there were no votes against and only two countries, China and Cuba, abstained).

This is not a novelty. Political rights are as old and as traditional as freedom rights. The French Revolution already claimed sovereignty for "la Nation" or the people. Art. 3 and 6 of the French "Déclaration" of 1789 stated:

> Le principe de toute souveraineté réside essentiellement dans la Nation. Nul corps, nul individu ne peut exercer d'autorité qui n'en émane expressément . . . La loi est l'expression de la volonté générale. Tous les citoyens ont le droit de concourir personnellement, ou par leurs représentants à sa formation.[1]

The right to democracy is the right of the people and of every member of the people to participate in the decisions of the government and in the framing of the laws. The underlying justification of this right is the wish of people to control their own lives. Few people are willing to accept that their lives are controlled by others.

Related to the principle of self control or self government is the claim that people can only be subject to those laws and decisions to which they agree. "[P]eople are obligated to obey the laws of government only insofar as people have consented to those laws, or to the power exercised in passing those laws".[2] If you have to obey laws you do not agree with, you do not control your own life. I will deal with the problem of the minority in just a few moments.

There are two ways of guaranteeing that the people agree with the rules they are supposed to respect. One way is to allow the people to make the rules themselves, for example by voting in a local meeting or in a referendum. The other way is to allow the people to elect or dismiss representatives who frame the rules. In the latter case, the people contribute indirectly to the framing of the rules because it is likely that they will on elect and re-elect representatives who frame rules according to their wishes. Participation or control can indeed be exercised on two levels: either directly or through the election or dismissal of representatives; election in the case of representatives who vote for the laws the people would also have voted for themselves, dismissal in the opposite case.

The principle of self control requires that everyone who is subject to the laws has the right to contribute to the framing of the laws. However, some-

---

1 Rials, S. 1982, *Textes constitutionnels français*, Paris: Presses Universitaires de France, p. 5.
2 Nelson, op. cit., p. 43.

thing more than a mere contribution seems to be required. Does self control imply that everybody agrees with the laws? That would mean that majority rule is unacceptable and that democracy in the sense of the rule of the people is necessarily a system of unanimous decisions. Is that possible or even acceptable? It is neither, because there will always be social divisions, and that is a good thing too. The will of the people is always the will of the majority. The will of the people does not stifle minority voices. Unanimous decisions are more characteristic of authoritarian regimes.

One could be inclined to think that a truly democratic system should be a system of unanimous decision, because only such a system gives everyone self control, respects the wishes of everyone and therefore respects the will of the people, the entire people and not just the majority. There is no frustrated minority that has to be coerced to abide by the decisions of the majority and that therefore loses self control. However, on the scale of large communities this would be practically impossible apart from exceptional circumstances. It would furthermore create a sinister sect-like situation of conformity and of choreographed manifestation of unity which we associate more with North Korea than with democracies.

This does not mean that unanimous decisions or decisions by a qualified majority are never desirable. In order to understand the practical problems linked to the choice between majority decisions and unanimous decisions, one has to look at the balance between on the one hand the costs paid by the minority as a consequence of the decision of the majority, and on the other hand the decision making costs or costs paid in order to be able to come to a decision. In a unanimous decision the former cost is zero because nobody suffers the consequences of other people's decisions, but the latter cost is very high because in most cases it is difficult or impossible to arrive at a unanimous decision. In a dictatorship, the opposite is true: it is very easy to arrive at a decision — much easier than to arrive at a majority decision — but the consequences, not only for the minority, may be very harmful.

The majority system of a democracy seems to strike a correct balance between both extremes by minimizing though not eliminating the elements of duty, coercion, frustration, cost and difficulty. If, however, in some cases the costs of a decision are very high — for example in the case of a decision affecting adversely some of the fundamental interests of a minority — then it can be acceptable to pay a higher decision making cost and try to find some kind of consensus.

Let us also note that the political rights cited above do not grant a right to be in control all of the time. They merely give the right to participate in the government. The will of the people mentioned in the articles is also undefined and there is no reason to believe that it refers to unanimity. Still, is it acceptable that the decision of a majority is described as the will of the "people"? Unanimity is apparently closer to the combined ideal of self government of the people and self government of the individual. It seems as though democracy can only be a real system of self government if every single individual member of the people is in agreement with every other individual member, because this is what we need if we want to have every individual's decision accepted and implemented. But then democracy is impossible. We will have to settle for something less.

If decisions are made by the majority instead of the unanimous people, then it seems to be impossible to claim that the people rule, govern or have power, and then there seems to be no self government for the people, only self government of the majority and its government over the minority. It is true that a majority system always implies the use of coercion towards the minority. The minority is forced to do something or to abstain from doing something, even if it wishes otherwise or its interests tell it to do otherwise. But this is the case even in a system of unanimous decisions. There is always a part of the people that rules another part, because there are always certain persons who are excluded (children, aliens, criminals, etc.). Furthermore, there is always the phenomenon of someone deciding to do "x" at a certain moment but having to be forced to do "x" at another moment and in other circumstances because at that time and place he rather believes in "y" (take the example of the alcoholic who promises to stop drinking, locks up the wine and throws away the key to force his future self to respect the decision of his present self; he is then governed by his own superior self[3]). So even unanimity does not exclude force or coercion.

The word "people" does not mean "everybody", because today's everybody is different or thinks in a way that is different from tomorrow's everybody, and because some people are by definition excluded. Furthermore, apart from the impracticalities it is not desirable to create a political system

---

3 Harrison, R. 1996, *Democracy*, London/New York: Routledge.

that always fulfills every desire. Not all desires are acceptable. Of course, it is good that as many people as possible can fulfill as many of their desires as possible. That is one of the justifications of democracy. With the exception of a system of unanimity, majority-democracy is the best way to achieve this. The majority of the people fulfill their desires, and everybody is now and then part of the majority, at least in a well functioning democracy. The minority, the group of persons supposedly living under the rule of the majority, is not a homogenous or unchanging group of persons. It always consists of other persons and this makes the yoke of the minority a bit easier to carry. And, in any case, the fundamental desires of the minority are always protected by its human rights, rights which the majority cannot violate.

MULTI-PARTY AND TWO-PARTY DEMOCRACY

If we understand self control or self government as being the goal of political rights, then it is tenable that majority-democracy, as a way to participate in government and to translate of the will of the people in government policy and laws, is the best way of making these rights *real*. However, as mentioned before, majority democracy can mean two things, representative democracy or direct democracy, and either of these terms can in turn mean many different things. So the question is: what kind of majority-democracy do we choose as the best means to make political rights *real*? Is a parliamentary system the best way to take the will of the people into account? And if so, a system of proportional representation or rather a district version, as used for example in the UK and to some extent also in the US? Is a multi-party parliamentary system better than a two party one? Or vice versa? Or perhaps we should complement a representative or parliamentary democracy with some kind of direct democracy?

Most democracies are multi-party representative democracies. However, we see that when there are more than two political parties competing for power, it often happens that no single party represents the majority. Therefore, party coalitions are necessary in order to establish a political majority and a government. The problem with coalitions is that they or their policies often do not represent the will of the majority of the people. These policies are not submitted to popular approval because they are decided after the election and on the basis of the balance of power produced by the election. After the election, different parties produce a coalition agreement based on their respective electoral strength. This agreement contains the basic government policy plans. The electorate cannot decide on the composition or policies of coalitions and hence they cannot decide on the political program and policy of the government either, because this program and policy are the result of post-election negotiations and agreements between the coalition partners. Government policy is not something that is proposed to the electorate before the election and then approved or rejected by the electorate. It is established only after the election and during negotiations between parties that bargain on the basis of their relative strength (their strength in turn is based on the election result). The voters never approve the results of these negotiations. Government policy is therefore not the execution of the will of the people — which should be the hallmark of democracy — but the execution of an agreement between political parties. It is obvious that this agreement can be quite different from what the people would approve.

Government coalitions (or organized majorities) are bound together by agreements and compromises between political parties. These agreements and compromises, which are the result of negotiations that take place after the elections (although sometimes political parties announce their alliances in advance), make up government policy. This policy is, by definition, unknown before the election and hence the electorate cannot express itself on this policy. Sometimes, these negotiations as well as their results are even hidden from the public and can result in the return to government of parties that have been decimated in the elections. It is possible that a voter would have voted for another party if he had known the result of the coalition negotiations in advance. If parties can return to power after losing an election, then they become untouchable. They do not have to fear losing an election, and hence the fear of losing can no longer ensure that they keep their promises, that they execute the policies that got them elected and that represent the will of their voters.

In a multi-party system, the voter does not even know the result of the election after the election has taken place. He has to wait for the result of the negotiations between parties and has no input at all in these negotiations. Only then is he informed about which government will take office and which government program will be implemented (and some parts of this program are often even hidden from the public). There is no direct election of the government and its policies, and the composition and the program of the government are unpredictable, even after the results of the election of parliament are known. In a democracy, the result of an election is, of course, always unpredictable, but in a multi-party system, this result remains unpredictable even after the election has taken place.

In a multi-party system, the government and the government policies are unpredictable because it is uncertain who will be part of the government. Even when this is known, it is often unclear what the parties have had to surrender in order to achieve the compromises necessary to forge the coalition and the government agreement. Furthermore, it is unclear which compromises will be necessary in the future in order to maintain the coalition. The voter cannot express himself on any of these compromises and agreements, even though they determine government policy. Government policy therefore cannot be the expression of the will of the people.

Election campaigns and government policies are by definition very different things in such a system. Politics loses its credibility and people stop participating because there is no link between cause and effect, between a vote or a party manifesto on the one hand and government policy on the other hand. Voters have practically no influence on the composition and the policies of the government. They can only express their disappointment afterwards, when it is too late. And there is no guarantee that new coalition negotiations take this expression into consideration. Democracy ceases to exist when citizens have no influence and when government policies reflect compromises between political parties rather than the will of the people.

Political parties and individual politicians suffer a loss of credibility. They need party coalitions because they seldom have an absolute majority. Consequently, they cannot implement their manifesto and election promises completely. In the best case, they can only implement a diluted version resulting from compromises with other ruling parties. In the worst case, these compromises force politicians to modify the policies that they have presented to the electorate. Ultimately, the loss of politicians' credibility and trustworthiness can affect the entire political system and even the concept of democracy in general.

The often-lamented discrepancies between promises and policies are, in part at least, the consequence of a multi-party system. This system makes it very difficult to execute the will of the people and therefore makes it difficult to preserve democracy and to make political rights *real*. The will of the people is translated into a number of votes for a number of party manifestos, but government policy is not the implementation of the manifesto with the majority of votes because there is only rarely such a majority manifesto in a multi-party system. Government policy is not even the implementation of a sum of different manifestos. It is the implementation of a negotiated compromise between different manifestos, a compromise moreover which is not subject to the approval of the electorate.

The multi-party system is of course not the only cause of discrepancies between election propaganda and government policies. Power politics, psychology, and the use of non-critical but high-emotion issues to divert attention from more fundamental policy differences, also play a role. Winning the election and profiting from the benefits of elected positions are often the only reasons why politicians formulate policies and promises. They often do not have the intention of effectively implementing these policies, not even when the system allows them to do so. They intend to pursue their self interest. This also diminishes the credibility of persons and institutions.

The lack of stability and decisiveness of coalition governments is another phenomenon that makes it difficult to execute the will of the people and that therefore undermines democracy, or, better, a certain kind of democracy. A coalition between different political parties can only result from a mix of different and often contradictory political ideologies and manifestos. The problem is that some things cannot be mixed. Some contradicting opinions cannot be harmonized into one compromise opinion and some opinions are so fundamental that every compromise is unacceptable. If, during the years in government, a problem related to these fundamental and conflicting opinions arises, then the politicians can act in different ways.

1. Decisions and even discussions regarding this matter are avoided or even prohibited by the coalition agreement. The advantage of such a strategy is the relative stability of the government. Coalitions do not break up because conflicts between opinions are excluded from the political agenda. The downside is that the government is indecisive and ineffective. Problems are not solved and the political parties lose their identity and their distinctive character. A party cannot implement its fundamental principles that distinguish it from other parties when these other parties are necessary partners in government and claim to protect other and incompatible principles. Parties

lose their attractiveness and credibility and citizens become indifferent. A related phenomenon is the so-called "move to the political center". All parties start to look alike. Vagueness does not encourage political participation and politics loses its attractiveness for citizens. They may decide to turn their backs to politics, which means that there is no longer a will of the people to implement. Political parties are seen as institutions that are more interested in safeguarding the government and thus their own power, than in preserving and defending fundamental ideological principles. Politics becomes a world of pragmatism and opportunism in which basic principles are given up for a seat in the government. Democracy loses its legitimacy.

2. If it is impossible to decide not to decide, and if everybody holds onto his initial ideological position, then there can be no decision. The coalition will most likely break up. The problem is not only indecisiveness but also instability. Citizens are not pleased if they have to elect a new government every year. Politicians are praised for their ideological purity, but this does not solve the problems. After all, the image of politicians is not more important than efficient decisions and stable government.

3. The last possibility is a compromise decision of some kind. Contrary to the two previous possibilities, there is now a decision, but it is a decision that pleases none of the parties involved because it corresponds to none of their fundamental principles. As in the first possibility, politicians are criticized for their ideological wavering.

A multi-party system is therefore often indecisive or unstable and this is another reason why it is very difficult to execute the will of the people (or even a leadership consensus on what would be best for the people, whether they realize it or not), in such a system. If a decision cannot be concluded because of differences in the coalition, or if the government is so unstable that there is no opportunity to decide, then the will of the people cannot be executed. The problem of the execution of the will of the people is not even a real problem because the vagueness of politics and its lack of credibility force people to turn away from politics altogether. They do not have a will anymore.

Indecisiveness is often a consequence of the pursuit of stability. Decisions are avoided because they can endanger the coalition and therefore the government. It seems that decisiveness and stability cannot go together in a multi-party system. The fear of instability not only leads to indecisiveness. It can also lead to extreme decisions. Sometimes, parties need the support of small and extremist parties in order to form a majority and a government. These extremist parties can blackmail the government by threatening to leave the coalition, to break up the majority and to bring down the government. These minorities can therefore force the government to take extreme decisions and they create a system of de facto minority rule.

So it seems that a multi-party representative democracy is not the best way to *realize* political rights. Does all this mean that democracy cannot work and has to be rejected? Not necessarily. Perhaps these problems can be solved within the framework of democracy. If we take a glancing look at one alternative, a two-party system as it is or was practiced in Great Britain or the US for example, then we notice that this system does not suffer the same drawbacks. In a two-party system, the winner of the election forms the government without further ado. The manifesto of one party becomes government policy and the majority of the people consciously choose government policy. The result of the election determines automatically and immediately the composition and the program of the government. There is a direct link between the votes and the government, and a party that loses the election cannot be part of the government. A two-party system clearly has some advantages:

1. In a two-party system, politicians do not have to decide independently on the composition and the policies of the government after the election has taken place. There is no need for compromise between political parties in order to create or maintain a coalition. The voters are not excluded from important decisions such as the choice of the parties that govern or the choice of the policies of the government. The voters decide who is part of the government and which party manifesto becomes government policy. The only thing they have to do is vote for one party or another.

2. Government policy is much more predictable because there is no need for compromise as a means to save the government and to avoid a break-up of the coalition. There is no need for compromise as a means to create a government either. Governments are not coalitions. Consequently, election

propaganda and government policies are more compatible and democracy retains its credibility.

3. Political parties can hold on to their ideological profile because they do not have to adapt their policies to the wishes of their partners. They can reach their goals, they can be decisive and efficient, and this means that they can keep their attractiveness. Politics itself remains attractive. On the other hand, if there are only two parties, these parties are bound to contain many different currents. This may limit their ability to take decisions and may force them to make internal compromises.

A two-party system can therefore solve some of the problems created by a multi-party system. However, one has to pay a price for this solution. As all things in life, a two-party system also has some disadvantages:

1. Choices are obviously limited in a two-party system. Instead of being able to choose between many different parties and ideologies, the voter can only choose between two parties. It is very difficult to represent all the different ideological currents when there are only two parties. However, the two parties in a two-party system can be heterogeneous and can incorporate different albeit related and compatible ideological currents. Unfortunately, this means reintroducing the problem of indecisiveness we find in multi-party systems. We are not likely to have a stable majority and a stable government able to take decisions when the governing party is internally divided on issues.

2. Changing the electoral system and introducing a threshold — for example a threshold limiting representation in parliament to parties that have more than 5% of the votes — is one of the ways in which to enforce a two-party system. Such a threshold, however, means limiting political equality. Not all voters are treated equally. Those who have voted for small parties are not represented. Their voices are not heard, their interests are not protected, and they have less or perhaps no influence on policies. Minorities are discriminated. History has shown that small parties can be very useful because they function as a stage for the appearance of new issues (the green parties for example). Large parties have often reacted positively and have incorporated these issues in their own manifestos. They probably would not have done so if small parties had not proven the existence of a grassroots interest

in these issues. If an issue can attract votes, even relatively few votes, then large parties will be interested, unless of course these votes do not count.

3. A threshold system makes it much more difficult for parties to grow. A party that is not represented cannot use parliament as a stage to show itself and to generate support. Therefore, there is a kind of exaggerated stability in politics.

4. The so-called "first-past-the-post" system combined with a system of election districts — whoever has most votes in a district (not necessarily the majority of votes) gets the seat in parliament reserved for this district and becomes the only representative for the district ("winner-takes-all") — is another way in which to enforce a two-party system. In some cases, this electoral system gives power to a relative majority and therefore not necessarily an absolute majority (a party that has a few more votes than all other parties in a majority of districts, will have a majority of seats in parliament, but perhaps a minority of the national votes). In fact, it can result in the rule of a minority. An important minority or maybe even a majority may not be represented at all. Again, political equality is limited and not everyone can enjoy political rights. There is no longer a match between the views of the people and the views present in parliament. A system of districts also limits political equality when the districts are not of the same size. If both a small group of people and a large group of people have one representative, then we can hardly claim to have political equality. (In some countries, rich minorities have often been given small districts that favored them politically and offered them a very large and disproportional share of the seats in parliament, a practice known as "gerrymandering"). However, I believe that some modifications can make the district system acceptable. There can be some kind of safety net for minorities failing to get represented (some kind of guaranteed representation for example). There can also be supplementary conditions for representation, in order to avoid giving power to relative majorities that are in fact absolute minorities.

DIRECT DEMOCRACY

So it is not so easy to choose between a multi-party and a two-party system. Therefore, it can be useful to look beyond representative democracy. Direct democracy does not have the disadvantages of either a multi-party system or a two-party system. In a direct democracy, the majority and the policies depend exclusively on the votes and not on coalitions, negotiations, districts, thresholds, etc. There is no problem of decisiveness or government stability either and there is no need to limit political equality. It is obvious that the problems posed by a multi-party system or a two-party system should not force us to reject democracy altogether but may force us to take another look at the long forgotten and often cursed tradition of direct democracy.

Another advantage of direct democracy is that it avoids some of the problems any kind of representative democracy faces when trying to implement the will of the people by way of votes for persons rather than issues. Citizens who engage in indirect participation can only influence decisions on issues and can never decide themselves. They can only decide on persons who will then decide on the issues. They elect only those rulers who are likely to decide an issue in a certain way, but this is never certain beforehand. The fact that afterwards the people can dismiss the rulers if they did not decide the issues in a satisfactory way, may force the rulers to comply, but this is not automatic. That is why citizens in an indirect democracy merely influence the decision on issues. They can only decide on issues in a direct democracy.

Representation is delegation. By giving my vote to a person, I yield my power to decide on issues. This person acquires the power to decide certain things in my place, things on which I no longer have a say. I can only agree or disagree with the decisions of my representative and I can only do this:

• Afterwards, when it may be too late, and

• For the whole of his decisions at once, not decision by decision.

I cannot agree or disagree with each decision separately, even though perhaps he took some good as well as some bad decisions. I can only vote for or against the whole person of the representative. This is not only a lack of finesse; it also reduces the power of the people to influence decisions and to judge politicians. A politician may take one very unpopular decision and still be re-elected, because all his other decisions are approved by the people. The people generally approve of the politician, and therefore cannot disavow the unpopular decision at the election. However, this means that decisions can be taken against the will of the people, and cannot be undone by the people. The people, therefore, do not have control over theirs lives. Or vice versa, this unpopular decision convinces people to vote against the politician, thereby undoing a lot of decisions they agree with.

In a representative system, it seems that the will of the people cannot be adequately expressed and implemented because the people cannot vote on every political decision separately, which means that the people do not rule and do not enjoy political rights. The people yield their power and are unable to enforce the adequate implementation of their will. The impossibility of issue-oriented choice rather than person-oriented choice creates the temptation to focus everything on the person of the politician. After all, that is the only thing left. When it is impossible, in a vote, to distinguish between good and bad deeds of the politician, then one is liable to focus on things as vague as personality, general convictions, charisma, image, etc. The people vote for or against politicians, names or faces, not for or against ideas or acts because they cannot use their votes to distinguish between different ideas or acts. The consequence is:

> a mesmerizing politics of media on which millions are spent to promote slick images and avoid substantive issues, in the name of providing an accountability that is also entertaining; it is a politics citizens watch rather than something they do.[4]

Direct democracy can move democracy away from a system for choosing and legitimizing (or dismissing) leaders without a clear reference to any specific content. It can create a system where the people can decide on issues and not just on the people who are supposed to decide the issues in their place. It is not without reason that representative democracy is often called leadership democracy. It is an instrument to choose the leaders and the rulers of the people. It is not a structure allowing the people to rule and govern themselves.

Representative democracy tends towards oligarchy or aristocracy. Power comes from the people but does not stay with the people. It is taken over by a limited number of persons standing above the people and forcing the people to be passive in between election days. The selection, dismissal and control of leaders, the only citizen activity allowed by representative democracy, tends to become an empty exercise in personality evaluation and to move away from content. Why monitor the individual actions of the politicians when, at the day of the election, it is impossible to pronounce a judgment on

---

4 Barber, op. cit., p. xii.

each action separately? When it is all or nothing, an intuitive understanding of the general line of political action is enough and this general line can be adequately understood by looking at the image, the character and the vision of the representative.

It seems, therefore, that representative democracy makes the *realization* of political rights very difficult if not impossible. In a representative democracy, the people are allowed to decide on who has the power to decide on issues. But how can they do this if they can only say "yes" or "no" to a person and not to the things this person has done? Do they have to make a sum of the good things and the bad things every representative has done or proposes to do, give a weight to every single action, and then choose the representative or the candidate with the best score? Even if they make these unlikely calculations, they will still choose persons who have done things or will do things they do not like. They will never be able to vote against these things, because at the next election their calculation will force them to vote again in favor of the same persons. They can never endorse or reject particular decisions of a representative and they can never give the signal that the representative should stop doing something which is contrary to the will of the people, except if they vote against the representative and thus against the good things he or she has done. The only correct judgment they can make is through non-political channels such as the media. There they can point to specific good or bad deeds without having to endorse or reject the entire person of the representative. The problem is that this kind of judgment, compared to a vote, may well be without consequences.

The people become passive spectators who can only correct the course of events in extreme cases, for example the case of the politician who hardly does anything in accordance with the will of the people. In every other case, the people have to throw away a lot of good things in order to get rid of some bad things, or keep some bad things for the sake of some good things. No wonder people become alienated.

The problem is, of course, how to separate cause and effect. Representative democracy often justifies itself by pointing to the passivity, apathy and lack of interest of citizens. No one asks the question whether this passivity — if it exists at all — is a consequence of the lack of opportunities to act in a representative system. If there were more possibilities for the citizens to act and influence decisions, for example by being able to disapprove of certain decisions, then the citizens would probably be much more active. If you cannot vote on issues which concern you and if the only choice left is one between personalities of politicians or one between general ideologies, then why take an interest in issues, why be passionate about politics? Why should you participate? If your opinions on specific matters and specific political decisions are of little consequence, as is the case in representative democracy, then why would you have such opinions in the first place? If, on the contrary, you know that your opinions can influence things and can perhaps undo certain mistaken political decisions, then you will have opinions and you will want decisions to conform to these opinions. Moreover, you will have a sense of responsibility because you know that what you think can be implemented. You will think twice and study the possible consequences of your thoughts. You will not permit yourself to think indiscriminately.

Only a regular dose of direct democracy can promote this kind of thinking, activity and responsibility. It has to be possible to let citizens vote in a referendum dealing with important decisions of the representatives. At the next election it may be too late or it may be impossible to distinguish the different important decisions and to come to a clear and balanced judgment on the record of the representative in question. An added advantage of this procedure is that it can help to thwart anti-politics. The citizens are themselves responsible and cannot shift responsibility for all kinds of wrongs to "politics" and "politicians who are all the same."

If people want to have control over their own lives — which I think most people want — then they have to understand that they must act themselves. They have to decide on issues and should not leave things to representatives. And acting means having responsibility for your actions. Citizens should not be represented for every decision, otherwise there is no self government.

A purely representative system robs citizens of their opinions, their sense of responsibility and their activity, and afterwards legitimizes itself by pointing to the lack of these things. If citizens lose their opinions, they also lose their sense of community and their community life. If you have opinions, you naturally want to convince other people of your opinions, you create communities and you guarantee not only an important human value but also one of the major prerequisites of democratic politics. This is another way in which representative democracy cuts off the branch it is sitting on.

> One of the mischiefs of representative government, which insists on governing for a citizenry to which it promises to be accountable, is that it robs individuals of common activities that could form a citizenry into a community. Even if a representative regime governs on behalf of its clients with efficiency, equitability, and due respect for popular liberty, it will impair rather than enhance the people's capacity for lateral public ties and community affection.[5]

An ideal democracy allows the people to influence decisions but also to decide for themselves now and again. The ability to control your own life depends on this. An ideal democracy is therefore a direct democracy, at least in part. People in a non-democratic regime also influence their leaders and influence therefore cannot be the main characteristic of democracy, although it is true that in a representative democracy the people have more influence than anywhere else. Influence in a representative democracy is more structured and more effective than in non-democratic regimes. However, this means that the difference between a representative democracy and other forms of government is merely a difference in degree, namely the degree of influence. The difference between a direct democracy and all other forms of government, including indirect democracy, is a difference in kind because the nature of participation is different. Instead of influencing the decisions of the government — which the people can do everywhere — the people in a direct democracy can decide for themselves. This gives the citizens a greater measure of control over their own lives and hence gives more *reality* to political rights.

Direct democracy is the decision making process in which the people themselves (or a part of the people for matters that only concern this part) take the decisions that affect their lives. A referendum and a council meeting are examples of direct democracy. Typical of direct democracy is the lack of separation between rulers and ruled, between official and unofficial political discussion. Politics is not something politicians do. Every citizen is a politician in a direct democracy.

Of course, direct democracy also has its disadvantages, which is why a mixed system, with some elements of different kinds of democracy, direct and indirect, is best. Disadvantages of each kind are then canceled out by the advantages of other kinds. Practically speaking, as most existing democracies are almost purely representative, we should strive to add some direct participation to these democracies. Then let us have a look at the disadvan-

---

5 Ibidem, p. 244.

tages of direct democracy so that we can implement this proposal in a reasonable fashion.

Direct democracy, as a system in which the people vote on issues and problems rather than on parties or persons, is very controversial. One often points to the risk of emotional reactions when the people are allowed to vote in a referendum on a certain problem. And although the same argument was used not so long ago against the right of women to vote for parliament, it is not a completely stupid argument. It is indeed not impossible that a majority of the people would vote to accept a certain kind of cruel punishment in a referendum held days after a gruesome series of murders.

However, is that a sufficient reason to reject the system of referenda? I think not, but we need to put some limits on referenda. For example, decisions taken by referendum cannot contradict the rights contained in the constitution, just as laws cannot. A constitutional court could for example be required to pronounce itself on the constitutionality of a referendum before it is allowed to take place. That will already limit the harm that can be done by referenda.

This requirement is not extravagant if you consider that referenda are one way to *realize* a particular human right. It would be inconsistent to allow referenda to violate other human rights. As stated before, rights should be balanced against each other and the exercise of one right cannot lead to violations of other rights. In my previous example, the right of the people to participate in government cannot violate the rights of criminals.

Another argument to counter the "emotionality thesis" could be that it is much easier for an individual or a small group to get overly excited about some issue then it is for an entire population. It is relatively difficult to excite the majority of a population at the same time and in the same way. The larger the group, the more diverse it will be.

A somewhat related argument against referenda is based on the possibility that elites or demagogues manipulate the people. However, it is rather strange to try to avert this danger by leaving politics entirely to elites, even elected elites. If elites manipulate the people, then it is because they want the people to decide something in a particular way. If the people can no longer decide through referenda, then the elite no longer needs to manipulate. But that does not make the problem go away. You cannot stem the fear of elites by giving all the power to the elites. Moreover, we should not underestimate the ability of the people to decide for themselves, independently of manipulation. And there are ways to limit manipulation, for example one can enforce the neutrality of the media, limit campaign expenses, etc.

What about the already mentioned apathy or indifference of the people? Or perhaps their lack of knowledge of complex political matters? Apart from the fact that the representatives of the people are not likely to be more knowledgeable than the people themselves — the people tend to get the representatives they deserve — there is also the educational aspect of participation in referenda. This participation enhances the ability to judge certain matters. If people are allowed to vote on a certain issue, then automatically there will be debates on the issue. People will follow these debates because they want to vote responsibly. During these debates, people will learn different arguments for and against a certain decision. If you know that you will never have a say on a certain matter, then you will not take the trouble of getting to know the matter. What would be the use? Knowledge of something, as well as an interest in something, comes with the power to decide on it. The apathy of the people, to the extent that it is a fact, is caused by disenfranchisement and by the knowledge that involvement and engagement will not have any influence on events. When there are referenda, people have influence and everything else, interest, knowledge, even passion, can follow. Participation in referenda indeed requires involvement and knowledge, but these preconditions are created in the process. They should not be demanded beforehand. The appetite comes while eating, as well as the sense of taste.

A final argument against referenda is that they simplify complex problems to a "yes-no" question. However, it is not clear why complex problems could not have a "yes-no" answer. What is clear is that some problems are rendered more complex than they are, perhaps to preserve some kind of expertocracy. Moreover, the answer in a referendum can be more complex than a mere "yes" or "no". There are more sophisticated techniques to organize a referendum. A referendum can be held in stages, for example. A "yes" answer to a first question may lead to subsequent questions. "If you accept that ..., would you also be willing to accept ... as a consequence of your choice?". Or: "If you accept that ..., but it turns out that a large minority has strong feelings against this, would you then accept a milder proposal such as ...?", etc.

DEMOCRACY AND NON-POLITICAL RIGHTS

We have now seen how democracy *realizes* political rights and which type of democracy is best suited for this purpose (a mixed system). But democracy is necessary for the protection and *realization* of civil or freedom rights as well. The legitimate existence of a continuous, open and public power struggle in which the entire people can participate (directly and indirectly), justifies and creates public conflict in general, in the society at large and in every domain of life. If conflicts between political opinions are allowed to appear in the public domain, then why should other public opinions be forbidden? Democracy institutionalizes publicity and freedom of speech because it promotes the public appearance of political opinions. The democratic power struggle justifies the free expression of opinions. The openness of democratic processes guarantees openness in society as a whole and in non-political matters. Politics functions as an example for the whole of social life.

This is another case of reverse causation: democracy promotes the freedom of expression but the freedom of expression also promotes democracy. There is no democratic power struggle without freedom of expression because this struggle requires criticism, argumentation and persuasion (in order to form majorities). In addition, democratic accountability, the public control of government actions, cannot function without respect for the right to free speech understood in the sense of the right to free flows of information. This meaning of the right to free speech is expressed in art. 19 of the Universal Declaration of Human Rights: "Everyone has the right to freedom of opinion and expression; this right includes freedom to hold opinions without interference and to seek, receive and impart information and ideas". This right allows the people to seek information, and as information on the workings of the government is not explicitly excluded, we must assume that it is included.

This is further proof of the link between democracy and human rights. The entire democratic process, including accountability and visibility of the government, necessarily requires respect for human rights, and not only free speech:

> without the guaranteed right of all citizens to meet collectively, to have access to information, to seek to persuade others, as well as to vote, democracy is meaningless. Democratic rights, in other words, are those individual

rights which are necessary to secure popular control over the process of collective decision-making on an ongoing basis.[6]

Human rights protect democracy, or, in other words, freedom rights *realize* political rights. Because freedom rights are prerequisites for a real power struggle, they are prerequisites for political rights and make these rights *real*. The participants in the power struggle have to be able to express themselves, to present themselves to the electorate, to create a distinct profile for themselves, and to make the electorate familiar with their political program (that is why they need the freedom of expression). They also have to be able to organize and associate in a group that is free from government control, because this allows them to gather strength and to have a more influential voice (so they need the freedom of association, the rule of law and the separation of state and society). And for the same reasons they have to be able to meet and demonstrate (so they also need the freedom of assembly).

Because democracy needs freedom rights, it tends to protect them. Hence, democracy is the form of government that is best placed to make these rights *real*. Freedom rights need democracy because democracy needs freedom rights. They are safer in a democracy because a democracy needs them. But a democracy also needs equal human rights. If not everybody has equal rights, there can be no equal influence, and if there is no equal influence, there can be no democracy. The creation of public opinion or of the will of the people depends on the equal influence of everybody or, in other words, on the equal ability to convince, and this equal ability requires equal human rights. Equal influence also requires respect for economic rights — because these rights limit the unequal influence of money on politics — and for the right to education for everybody — a right that limits the unequal influence of intellect or talent on politics.

All human rights must be respected simultaneously in order to have a proper democratic process. Many tyrannies allow the existence of opposition groups and even sometimes a limited degree of political participation, but these groups are ineffective because they do not have equal access to publicity, because they do not have the freedom to organize as they wish, or because the people lack the material or intellectual resources necessary to be able to choose wisely among candidates.

---

6 Beetham, op. cit., p. 190.

Democracy and human rights cannot function separately. They need each other and reinforce each other. Where you have one, you tend to have the other as well. And where you have one without the other, there is something missing in what you have. A democracy without human rights is not an ideal democracy, because it cannot function adequately. Human rights without democracy are not complete because one of the most important uses of human rights — calling into question the work of the government and creating a common point of view on the work of the government — is not allowed, or, if it is allowed, does not have any useful consequences because it is impossible to have a democratic vote. Human rights are not politically or ideologically neutral. They require democracy and are required by democracy. This again supports the statement (see Chapter 2) that human rights are not something primarily directed against politics or a way to limit politics. They are an essential part of democratic politics.

At first sight, there are some persistent facts that seem to contradict the statement that democracy and human rights are necessarily linked to each other. Democracies can apparently exist without respecting human rights (or all human rights), and human rights (or certain human rights) can apparently be respected by non-democratic regimes. An example of the former is of course the ancient Greek "polis" where human rights indeed did not exist, although the "polis" did guarantee a kind of freedom of speech, not for humanity as such but for a tiny minority of privileged citizens. It is clear however that the "polis" was not a democracy as we understand it today. It was an oligarchy in which the large majority of the people were excluded from politics. And although the word "democracy" was invented in the "polis", it is difficult to maintain that the people ruled the "polis". Inside the oligarchic group, decisions were made democratically based on freedom of expression and equality, but freedom and equality never became human rights, to wit rights belonging to human beings in general, including those human beings excluded from politics. Today only those states, in which the participants in the political decision making process are the same people as those who are subject to the political decisions, can be called democratic. In the Greek "polis", self government was only a reality for a small minority; the decisions of this minority governed the actions of the large majority of women, aliens and slaves.

Some present-day states such as the Islamic Republic of Iran regularly hold reasonably fair elections but hardly respect human rights. The question is, of course, what these elections are worth without the free expression of opinions, without free and open discussions among citizens regarding the record of the government and the most appropriate government policies, without free flows of information concerning the work of the government, without the freedom to associate and to form opposition movements, etc. Even in those countries in which people can vote for existing opposition movements (for example, Malaysia and Singapore), there is rarely a "rotation in office" because human rights are not respected and opposition movements are systematically sabotaged (they suffer from unjustified lawsuits, they do not have equal access to the media, etc.). Of course, the absence of a change of power does not prove that there is no democracy. The people can always decide the same thing. The problem is that the people cannot decide without human rights. A decision that is not based on free and open discussion, free flows of information and free association and assembly is not a democratic decision.

Hong Kong, before the last-minute democratic reforms implemented by the British government before it was returned to China, was considered a non-democratic state that respected a great number of human rights. In this case, the question is what these human rights are worth if they cannot be applied to or can have no consequence for the workings of the government. If you express an opinion, you expect some consequences resulting from this expression. Otherwise, it would be better not to express the opinion at all. What is the use of being able to express opinions on the workings of the government if this expression is entirely without consequences?

Respect for human rights will most probably lead to democratization. People who have freedom of expression will start to claim the right to vote. They will have opinions on the workings of the government and they will want to see these opinions implemented. Conversely, the presence of a partially democratic form of government will lead to the institutionalization of human rights. If the people can vote and therefore express themselves on things as important as the government, what is the use of prohibiting the expression of other kinds of opinions?

The transition of a rights regime to a democracy, or vice versa, is of course not as easy as all this seems to imply. A non-democratic government, even though it is kind enough to grant its people a few rights narrowly defined, will cling to power and will have the means to do so. It will resist demands for more democracy. The opposite seems to be easier. Democracies are more inclined to grant rights. Granting rights is also easier than changing the form of government, at least at first sight. Creating the institutions necessary for the enforcement of rights can also be an awesome task.

One can only maintain that there are democracies that do not respect human rights, or that there are non-democratic regimes that respect human rights, if one adopts some kind of reduced definition of either democracy or rights. An ideal democracy cannot exist without rights, and vice versa.

Chapter 10. Sovereignty and Intervention

New Sovereignty

In this chapter I will investigate the strange paradox between two important but contradictory concepts that can be used to help make rights and democracy real, namely national sovereignty and international intervention. Both these terms have always had some negative connotations from the point of view of human rights. These days, when we think of international intervention we can see only failure: when intervention was needed in Darfur or Rwanda, none was forthcoming. When there was intervention in Kosovo, the victims among the Serbs rather than the beneficiaries among the Albanians come to mind, and the aftermath only opens more questions about the wisdom (or long-term strategic interests) of outsiders promoting the dismemberment of a nation. The invasion of Iraq, justified partly on the basis of a proclaimed desire to install democracy over there, has instead resulted in a spreading circle of anarchy and destruction. We on the outside may believe a "dictator" is wrongly using claims of "sovereignty" as a shield against legitimate intervention, as a legalistic tool for self defense; however, an international "intervention," even in the name of imposing a certain view of rights, in fact must have other repercussions as well, at a minimum upsetting the social relations within a country and shifting its economic and cultural relations. And any country subjected to such intervention must always suspect that it is just an attractive cover story for a campaign to undermine a state.

Promoters of human rights, though, often see claims of "sovereignty" as a weapon in the hands of their enemies. They fail to see the possibility of sovereignty as an instrument for the protection of human rights. However, if sovereignty can be redefined, such a possibility does exist. Sovereignty is, in the minds of many, the complete freedom of the state from other, foreign states to do as it likes within its territory. Instead of this notion of complete freedom, we should focus on the notions of territorial integrity and political independence present in the concept of sovereignty. A state has a right to its sovereignty because the territorial integrity and political independence of a state are requirements for the self government of its people, and hence for democracy. A state that is the sole and highest authority in its territory creates and protects a political space and political institutions in which the people as a nation can shape their own common life, free from the interference and aggression of external powers. These institutions ideally also include federal and decentralized institutions protected by the nation state against outside aggression.

It is far from clear how democracy can be organized on a world level or even on a local level outside of state institutions and without state protection. And democracy seems to require that things that can be done locally must be done locally. Democracy at the local level diminishes the number of participants and hence increases the importance and the influence of each individual, which from a democratic point of view is a good thing. However, to promote precisely this maximization of the importance and the influence of the individual, in our globalized world, some problems require international and even global cooperation. In the second part of this chapter, I will come back to this problem and I will discuss how this cooperation can be organized in a democratic way.

Human rights as well still depend on the nation state for their effective enforcement. There are more or less effective international monitoring and judicial systems, but as yet no international or global enforcement mechanism for human rights. And in many cases this is not even desirable. Judicial processes, like democratic ones, are best carried out close to the people concerned. We do not want to go to The Hague in order to achieve judicial satisfaction on every human rights issue. We want our own judges to help us, and they will also be more familiar with our situation, closer to the perpetrators of an alleged crime, and hence more likely to be able to assess the case and, if appropriate, impose effective punishment. If human rights depend on the nation state, then this state has to be the sovereign power inside its territory, able to enforce judgments on human rights violations and in possession of the monopoly of violence (violence is sometimes necessary for enforcement). Of course, not all states are willing and able to provide local judicial protection, and then international protection is necessary. But national sovereignty should be the starting point.

Although it is possible and certainly also desirable to protect human rights and to organize democracy on a level that is higher than that of the state — but not at the expense of democracy and human rights protection at the state level[1] — human rights and democracy still require national independence and sovereignty. A state has to be sovereign, independent and free from interference and aggression if it wants to be able to guarantee human rights and democracy within its territory. If another state or group of states attacks an independent state and takes away its sovereignty, then we may see the end of human rights and democracy in both places. An aggressive state usually does not feel bad about rights violations, at home or in the land it has attacked; democracy is, after all, a people determining their own fate and is therefore incompatible with foreign occupation or interference. On the other hand, interference may be necessary for the protection of democracy and human rights. I will come back to this in a moment.

Sovereignty is especially important because democracy and human rights require it. But some adaptation of international law is required. Currently every recognized state, the most democratic as well as the most tyrannical one, has a far-reaching legal right to protect its sovereignty. This makes it difficult to intervene in order to promote democracy and respect for human rights, which is why the concept of sovereignty has fallen in disrepute and has been attacked from a moral point of view.

---

1 It is not impossible to imagine the current nation states as some kind of decentralized units of a future global federal state. Just as the municipalities or federal units of current federal states do not have to relinquish their democratic organization of local matters, there is no reason to believe that some form of democracy for the nation state level has to disappear when more and more matters are regulated and organized on a regional or global level. One can only hope that this regional or global level will also be organized in a democratic way, at least in a more democratic way than is the case today.

We need a new sovereignty, a transformation of the concept of sovereignty which allows for the possibility of international intervention in the case of egregious rights violations. Rather than an absolute right to sovereignty states would have a limited right. If intervention is justified, as it apparently would have been in the case of Rwanda, for example, sovereignty should give way. The problem of course is who is to decide, and on what basis, when such action is justified. If external interference is not justified then states must have the means to repel it and to protect themselves.

A non-democracy defending itself against external attempts to transform it into a rights-respecting democracy should have some difficulty to claim its right to sovereignty. However, given the dangers involved in intervention, even a non-democracy or a regime systematically violating human rights has a point when it acts to defend itself against intervention. The cure may be worse than the disease. Indeed, the kinds of intervention that are chosen in order to attempt to transform states into rights-respecting democracies ought to be proportional to the gravity of the situation in the target-country. When these attempts are disproportional, the target state can justifiably invoke its right to sovereignty as a means to repel these attempts. For instance, war, occupation and attacks on the territorial integrity of states in order to protect human rights can only backfire.

But some states try to use their sovereignty even against proportional international interventions to promote human rights and democracy, such as diplomacy or condemnations. They in fact believe that even the most superficial form of intervention or even public comment is illegal and that even the most horrendous violations of human rights do not warrant intervention. Regarding the current status of international law, they are probably right. Instead, some voices are calling for a new system of sovereignty which could give states only a conditional right to sovereignty, a sovereignty that could be overridden by the international right to intervention. The instruments of intervention and hence the limitations on sovereignty would vary according to the gravity of the situation. In the worst situations (government-sponsored genocide, for instance), sovereignty would completely give way: the right to self protection, independence and territorial integrity implicit in the notion of sovereignty would become null and void and a war and occupation would be justified. In less severe cases, only a part of sovereignty will give way. A country would be forced to allow inspections or to accept certain reforms, for example.

INTERVENTION

In this new sovereignty, there will be no absolute protection against interference but only a relative protection, a protection against disproportional and unjustified interference. Intervention is necessary because states do not always use their sovereignty, in the sense of their authority within their territory, in order to redress rights violations occurring in their territory. Sometimes, the state itself is the violator and it does not have the will to correct itself. In other cases, it may not have the appropriate mechanisms (i.e., division of powers) or the ability to correct itself. Outside pressure in the form of some kind of intervention would then be reckoned as necessary.

However, the main problem is the justification of intervention. How is this established? It seems that one condition is multilateralism. States cannot unilaterally decide that they should intervene elsewhere for the protection of rights or democracy. There has to be some global consensus. And the consensus must be built on legal and moral arguments, without being blocked by inconvenient factors such as the target nation being a strategic ally or the desire to keep one's own troops out of harm's way. Another condition, already mentioned, is proportionality. Furthermore, the possible negative effects of intervention should be taken into account and the effectiveness of less extreme measures tested to the full.

This limited sovereignty is still not entirely accepted in international law. The famous or infamous article 2 paragraph 7 of the United Nations Charter explicitly prohibits every intervention or violation of the sovereignty and territorial integrity of any UN member state, even the worst tyranny:

> Nothing contained in the present Charter shall authorize the United Nations to intervene in matters which are essentially within the domestic jurisdiction of any State.

This article is often used against attempts to intervene for the sake of human rights or democracy. Even merely verbal criticism of rights violations is often supposed to be the type of "intervention" prohibited by art. 2 par. 7. The "matters" referred to in the article are never precisely defined, so that every state is free to define them. Hence, intervention is practically impossible.

However, it is internationally accepted that some acts clearly do not belong to these "matters": violations of international law, attacks on international peace, and systematic and extreme violations of human rights if these violations threaten international peace. Chapter VII of the Charter allows Security Council intervention in these cases, and art. 2 explicitly provides an exception for this kind of intervention:

> [T]he doctrine expounded in San Francisco in 1945, by the framers of the UN Charter, to the effect that "if rights and freedoms were grievously outraged so as to create conditions which threaten peace or to obstruct the application of the provisions of the Charter, then they cease to be the sole concern of each State".[2]

This is important for human rights, although many violations of rights do not or not immediately threaten the peace. However, today's legal consensus on the definition of "matters" may even include violations unrelated to threats to peace. Again some human rights activists see that some "internal matters," which do not threaten the peace at first sight, can benefit from art. 2 par. 7, and demand intervention as these matters are perceived as clear violations of human rights and the Charter, which stipulates that the UN should protect human rights. The UN is seen thus not only a peacekeeping institute. Such people believe that the UN can and should take measures under Chapter VII (sanctions or even military intervention) against rights violations irrespective of threats to the peace. Chapter VII can override art. 2 par. 7 and efforts are being made to widen its application.

However, there is still some legal dispute on this matter and there is a view that we should adhere to a wide ranging and uniform interpretation of sovereignty, one that would continue to allow rights violations as long as they do not threaten the peace. This view holds that it is illegal to act in a way which would dismember or impair, totally or in part, the territorial integrity or political unity of sovereign and independent States conducting themselves in compliance with the principles of equal rights and self determination of peoples and thus possessed of a Government representing the whole people belonging to the territory without distinction of any kind.[3]

If a new definition of sovereignty can be agreed, a sovereignty not standing in the way of action to stop the worst rights violations, then, the rights

---

2 Cassese, A. 1992, *International Law in a Divided World*, Oxford: Clarendon Press, p. 161.
3 Vienna Declaration and Program of Action 1993, Adopted by the World Conference on Human Rights, doc UN A/CONF.157/23.

activists believe, the powers of the Security Council may need to be recon-sidered. Many interventions which would already be justified both morally and legally, under current international law, are blocked by the veto. This remains a crucial tool to avoid having one nation and its allies strong-arm the rest of the world; but it is also a means by which one nation and its allies can hold the world hostage to their collision of interests against the rest of the world.

Globalization

Many problems are no longer limited to the territory of a single state and are therefore difficult for states to solve independently. These problems are beyond the power of the so-called sovereign and independent state, no matter how powerful this state, and require international collaboration. All states have thus become interdependent. The US, for instance, is economi-cally and militarily very powerful, but depends on the oil-producing coun-tries for its energy, on the World Trade Organization for its trade interests, on its neighbors for controlling illegal immigration and drug traffic, on Is-lamic countries for its struggle against terrorism, etc. At the time of the Cold War, it depended for its security on the traditional balance of power theory, but also on international agreements, principally with the USSR, regarding limitations on military capacity. With the rules on limited capacity came the right to international inspection of this capacity, also a limit on sovereignty.

Many things have ceased to be purely internal matters. International collaboration means that different countries decide to tackle a problem together. International problems require international solutions. In some cases, states have created international institutions to help them solve in-ternational problems. The UN for instance was created to solve the problem of international aggression. NATO was created to defend the West against communism. States voluntarily hand over some of their powers and sover-eignty to such international institutions. These institutions can often take binding decisions without the consent of each individual member state. In any case, they establish certain common international rules and it is in the interest of the member states to abide by them because there is no solution without these rules. For example, states try to harmonize the rules on labor conditions or the levels of tax burdens in order to avoid de-localization and outsourcing. Or they try to find ways to impose stricter rules for the control of nuclear reactors in order to avoid international nuclear disasters or arms proliferation.

No state can well afford to close its doors, to refuse to communicate and cooperate. If it does, it will be unable to solve some of its most important problems. The time of *communitates superiorem non recognoscentes* (communities not recognizing any superior authority) is over. States can no longer be absolutely sovereign. The circumstances have created a general acceptance of international rules and institutions.

And growing interdependence has resulted in growing international influence. A state that depends on other states for solutions to its most pressing problems and that benefits from cooperation cannot pretend to be deaf when these other states demand that it stops violating human rights. It is no coincidence that states with the worst human rights record often also try to be autarkic (take North Korea, for instance). International opinion becomes more important as international collaboration becomes more important. The shield of sovereignty loses its strength and can no longer be used to counter criticism of human rights violations, because it is precisely the reality that sovereignty is already diminished that forced the states to cooperate. In a relationship of interdependence, states can also apply pressure on one another, can use sanctions, and deny assistance and collaboration. The more a state is economically dependent on other states, for example, the more it is exposed to economic measures that may be designed to pressure it to respect human rights. The downside is that small states are far more susceptible to pressure than large ones. But even large states are not invulnerable. Another problem is that states can also use their influence and pressure for other purposes than the promotion of human rights and democracy. That is another reason to prefer intervention by international institutions, and measures short of actual invasion.

All in all, it is good to see that sovereignty loses some of its power in favor of democracy and international human rights law, a part of international law moreover that is no longer based exclusively on consent but also on pressure and enforcement made possible by international law and interdependence. The moral boost that one would like to see in a new kind of sovereignty may result more or less automatically from the transformation of sovereignty that is already taking place in the real world. "[I]nterdependence could over time provide as effective a backing to regulation as outright force".[4] Force, fear or moral conviction are not the only reasons why people or nations choose to respect human rights. The fact that other states or international institutions use mutually beneficial cooperation mechanisms against a state may also be convincing. For example, it has become acceptable to ask that respect for human rights is a condition for the entry into these mechanisms (take the example of the European Union).

So it seems that it is not entirely true to say that treaties without a "sword" are mere words. There are many different ways to pressure states into compliance and the sword is only one of them. Enforcement, traditionally the weakest part of international law, seems to have become easier in a globalized world, although in a way that people from the time of swords would have been unable to imagine. It is much harder now to violate international rules or to ignore international condemnations than it was fifty years ago. Human rights law is becoming more and more effective.

The globalization of the world can make it easier to intervene for the sake of human rights and democracy, and it can also justify such intervention. Violations of rights in one country can easily affect other countries (refugee problems, the centripetal and centrifugal force of a civil war, the ripple effect of an economic crisis caused by bad governance). These other countries have a right to protect their interests, including by trying to protect human rights elsewhere.

But the facts may not move towards the desired goal so automatically. New sovereignty can be promoted by globalization, but globalization can also harm democracy. And if it harms democracy, it harms new sovereignty. New sovereignty is designed to give protection to the sovereignty of the people, but globalization often renders the sovereignty of the people quite meaningless. The power deflation experienced by the states vis-à-vis the market, multinational corporations, the environment and each other means that decisions affecting the well-being of the people are taken by outside forces (the market, companies, other states). It is obvious that this is incompatible with democracy and with the sovereignty of the people. Democratic control over events is an important value, but one that implies the presence of a state and a population capable of imposing its will. If a state cannot impose its will, as is shown by many problems of globalization, then we have to look beyond

---

4 Beetham, op, cit., p. 5.

the level of the state. International institutions can sometimes solve problems that are beyond the power of one individual state and one people.

International institutions are created in order to solve problems. Hence, they are created to give back power and control to a group of states and an association of different nations that have lost their individual power and control. Control and power are the reasons behind the creation of international institutions. And in a democracy, control and power mean sovereignty of the people and self government. It is therefore inconsistent to organize international institutions undemocratically. The rescue of self government and democracy — which is necessary because democracy can become meaningless on a state level when the state is confronted with international problems — is precisely the purpose of international institutions. New sovereignty as a concept should include the attempt to restore the sovereignty of the people at an international level. Self government is part of the justification of new sovereignty on the national level, but this new sovereignty should also protect the self government and the sovereignty of associated peoples on the international level. International institutions should not lead to a loss of self government for the different nations that they encompass because these nations join the institutions precisely to regain their self government.

But how do we organize the sovereignty or the self government of groups of nations on an international level? Many international institutions currently suffer from a lack of democratic accountability and legitimacy. It is quite easy to imagine states or their representatives working together in these institutions in order to solve international problems. But it is much more difficult to find ways in which different nations or peoples can work together. These nations have to keep some kind of participation and decision power in international institutions, otherwise we find ourselves in the same situation as the one created by multinational corporations generating nuclear waste, for instance: decisions that affect the people are not taken by the people. The people do not have their fate in their own hands. International institutions are created to remedy this lack of self government and should therefore, for the sake of coherence, be organized democratically. No external power should decide a people's fate, no market, no other states, but no international institution either. An international institution should not be an external power.

The problem is that international institutions comprise many states and many nations and it is often very difficult to frame a harmonious popular will overlapping all these nations. Is democracy possible at a level that is higher than that of the state? Democracy is not at its best on a large scale. Efficient participation is difficult in very large groups. On the other hand, international cooperation can stop events taking place without the agreement of the people. If we have international cooperation, we can avoid the situation in which one country or the market takes decisions that have negative effects elsewhere (for example, the decision to build a nuclear plant just at the border with another country, without involving the people of this other country; or the decision of one country to destroy its rainforests, irrespective of the consequence for the global climate). International cooperation has a positive influence on self government because it allows nations to control events that they individually would not be able to control.

It is obvious that international organizations, set up to solve international problems, must be democratic, at least when we remember that democracy and self government are among the reasons for solving international problems. Some of these problems inhibit self government because an individual nation is not able to deal with them. International organizations are set up to recreate self government by solving problems that inhibit self government. One should not create an undemocratic international institution, because the purpose of such an institution is precisely self government.

But how can we make existing international organizations more democratic? There are not many examples to inspire us. In any case, the people of the different states have to be represented in these organizations and not only in their own states. Direct democracy is also a possibility. Perhaps we can presume that we have a democratic decision from the moment that democratic states, in their position of members of the organization, take a common decision. These states represent their people and hence the people are indirectly involved in the decision. However, do these states have to decide unanimously? Or can we also apply the system of majority rule at an international level? In the latter case, we put aside entire nations. Is this acceptable? It is certainly not acceptable for the nations concerned. The reason why these nations joined the organization in the first place, was to solve problems that escaped their power and to recapture their sovereignty. They will never accept to be outvoted.

But then again, the people of every individual state do not have power when they are outvoted minorities in a larger entity, but the "people" of the whole have more democracy because they are now able to solve problems they were not able to solve when they were still divided. We accept the existence of minorities in state level democracies, so why not in international "democracies"?

The fact that international institutions take away a part of the sovereignty of states in order to be able to solve certain problems, does not have to imply a weakening of democracy. On the contrary, it can imply the rescue of democracy, on the condition of course that these institutions are governed democratically. Large-scale international cooperation is not per se undemocratic. True, it is much more difficult to organize it democratically. Small groups have the advantage of allowing more people to participate and of giving each individual more influence and control, and the smaller the better. The nation state is obviously less democratic than a town meeting. But larger groups have the advantage of being able to solve certain problems where small groups cannot. If democracy means determining one's own life, then it also means being able to decide something and to solve problems. A small group may enable everybody to speak but it cannot solve some of the major problems of life. A larger group may force people to participate less and to have less influence, but in effect such a group may be more democratic than a smaller group because its capacity to cope with certain matters is greater. This counters the argument that democracy is only appropriate for small groups in pre-modern societies.

CHAPTER 11. FREEDOM AND EQUALITY

FREEDOM VS. EQUALITY

This concludes the discussion of the system of human rights and the means to make rights real. One thing that has been presupposed and taken for granted until now is the importance of human rights. I already mentioned that it is not my intention to deal with this topic within the limits of this volume, but it seems unfair to avoid the question altogether. Why are human rights so important that we need to know how to make them real? Why do we need to understand them? My lapidary answer until now has been that human rights protect a number of universally important values such as peace, prosperity, freedom, equality, diversity, identity and belonging. What I failed to say is how they can do that. I think one can agree that an in-depth answer to such a question merits a separate discussion. And indeed I can point to another publication dealing only with this question.[1] What I can offer in the space of this book is just one example. In this chapter I will try to show how human rights can protect freedom and equality, two values which I think are universally important and cherished.

Over the last centuries, it has become kind of a tradition to juxtapose freedom and equality and to view these two important human values as almost tragically opposing goals, one inevitably leading to the limitation of the

---

1 See note 2.

other. For example, one can point to the way in which the claims of equality, as they are expressed in economic rights and income-redistribution, limit the freedom of the wealthier parts of the population. Moreover, the struggle against poverty has often become the overriding preoccupation and even an excuse for violations of freedom rights. Non-economic injustices are often readily accepted once people are convinced that these injustices are needed to combat economic injustices. Another example of the way in which the struggle for equality limits the freedom of certain groups is given by some kinds of affirmative action programs. And finally, the principle of non-discrimination may require limiting the freedom of expression of those who promote racism or other forms of discrimination.

Conversely, freedom can also limit equality. The unfettered free market tends to produce economic inequalities. When the unequal distribution of talent and starting-capital is not checked by government intervention then the outcome tends to be more economic inequality. In most cases, economic equality as prescribed by economic rights is not the automatic product of voluntary caritas or free solidarity. There is no Invisible Hand. Freedom alone does not guarantee economic equality. It often even diminishes it. Some kind of government intervention and coercion is necessary in order to redistribute wealth. An absolute protection of property — a freedom right — threatens economic equality. Another example: if absolute freedom of expression includes the protection of hatred and racist speech, then this can lead to inequality, discrimination and even genocide.

Unlimited and Limited Negative Freedom

Contradictions between cherished goals always have something tragic. Much of our great literature since the Greek tragedies deals with such contradictions (love and loyalty, duty and love, family and loyalty, love and faith, etc.). My thesis is that the contradiction between freedom and equality is caused by a certain way of understanding freedom and that the only way out of our tragedy is the adoption of a more complex and complete definition of freedom.

The definition which I want to object to has been most clearly stated by Thomas Hobbes in the following excerpt of his Leviathan:

> By LIBERTY, is understood, according to the proper signification of the word, the absence of externall Impediments: which Impediments, may oft take away part of a mans power to do what hee would.[2]

This definition of freedom as the ability to do what you want, has entered the common sense understanding of the word. It is a negative definition because it focuses on the absence of impediments, constraints or limits on actions (limits imposed by other human beings, by the state, by nature or perhaps even by our own passions). It is obvious that an absolute version of this kind of freedom is possible only outside of the state and the law.

However, is it possible at all? And if so, is it acceptable? For some of us it may be possible. It is not possible for the many victims who are the inevitable result of this kind of freedom. If everybody can do as he or she likes, then we create offenders and victims and only the offenders are free. Victims obviously cannot do as they like. And we can all become victims. Not even the strongest among us can do as he likes, because he has to sleep now and again and we are weak when we sleep. Unlimited and lawless freedom as in the definition of Hobbes cannot and should not exist. It is self destructive and immoral, as Hobbes himself by the way clearly understood.

Only anarchists still believe in this kind of freedom, which is license rather than liberty. Libertarians, proponents of the minimal state, free marketeers and liberals in the European sense of the word adopt a limited version of the Hobbesian freedom. They rightly worry about the victims and they agree to have laws which limit freedom for the sake of security and hence for the sake of the freedom of others. No freedom without security. They try to equalize freedom.

Freedom for them is always freedom in the state and freedom within the limits of the rule of law. In a situation of lawlessness, I can only do as I like if I am the strongest of all, which is very unlikely. Without laws, there is no freedom for all. If I accept the law, then I will gain security, survival and limited freedom. If I do not accept the law, then I will only create the freedom of the fox in the chicken-house, and I will probably not be the fox.

According to this school of thought, all coercion is bad but some kind of coercion is necessary. If people were always friendly to each other, the state would not be necessary and people would not have to accept a limitation of

---

2 Hobbes, T 1984, *Leviathan*, Harmondsworth: Penguin, p. 189.

their freedom. State coercion in the form of laws limits freedom because it forces people to act in a way that is contrary to their wishes. In this world-view it is accepted that coercion can actually promote freedom. Coercing one person and thus limiting his or her freedom can promote the freedom of other persons, namely the freedom of the "chickens".

However, because of the importance of freedom as the ability to do as you like, the proponents of limited negative freedom want to keep the area of the law and the state as small as possible. Liberalism, if we may use this term as a label for these people,[3] believes that the only way in which the state can promote freedom is by guaranteeing the security of the weak. The state should only protect the weak against the strong. In this way, it makes it possible for the weak to do as they want. It puts the freedom of the weak on the same and equal level as the freedom of the strong who can do what they want even without protection.

For the rest, the state should not do anything and should keep itself as inconspicuous as possible. It should create an area which is free from state coercion and in which people can do as they like. In a certain sense, this freedom is a stateless freedom even though the state must act to protect it. The area of non-interference must be as large as possible in order to allow freedom to become as comprehensive as possible. Freedom and politics can only go together because and insofar as politics guarantees freedom from politics.[4]

Contrary to anarchists, liberals believe — correctly, I think — that the area of freedom or noninterference cannot be unlimited because this would result in insecurity, chaos and war. But in a sense both anarchism and liberalism believe in unlimited freedom. For the former it is an ideal for the future, for the latter it is something which belongs to a perhaps mythical past (the time of the "contract") and which can only be desirable in the unlikely event that human beings learn to behave and to respect each others security.

Liberalism thus creates a separation between the unfree area of the state and the law on the one hand, and the free area of the rest of life on the other hand. I will object to this separation and will claim that the state can be an area of freedom and that involvement in the state can promote freedom.

---

3 Libertarians seems too narrow a term given the marginality of this school of thought compared to the widely held view on freedom which I try to describe here.

4 Arendt, H 1994, *Tussen verleden en toekomst*, Leuven: Garant, p. 79.

EQUAL FREEDOM

Is the problem of freedom and equality solved by liberalism? Law and the security that it produces indeed equalize freedom. But are our values really harmonized and is the tragedy resolved? Not quite. I can see at least three problems remaining. The first one is poverty. Poor people can't do what they want and the laws which protect their physical security against the free actions of other will not help them. Their situation is not primarily caused by the limitations imposed on them by the actions of others. And the provision of social security is much more controversial than the provision of physical security, which is bizarre given that both kinds of security have the same purpose, namely the equalization of freedom in the sense of the ability to do as you want. We see here that the state, by intervening and reducing poverty, can promote freedom.

A second problem with the limited Hobbesian freedom is revealed by the bigot. Take the example of the bigot who isn't poor but doesn't want anything else in life than watching sport, drinking beer and shouting to his wife. He can do as he wants, but is he free? Here we see that it may be necessary to redefine freedom and not only to limit it. Freedom means not only the ability to do what you choose, but also, and in the first place, the fact of having significant choices, the ability to expand the options you can choose from, the ability to make an educated choice between examined options and to choose the options which are best for yourself and for the people around you. In other words, freedom is the ability to choose the options which make ourselves better persons and allow us and our fellow-humans to self develop.

Now, how do you widen the available choices, and check if what you want is really what you want? Only if all possible options and choices are flooded with the light of publicity and education. When you see which options are available, when you hear people discussing the merits of different options and objects of volition, only then can you make an educated choice. This publicity, and hence freedom as the possibility to develop your self, requires a legal system. Legally protected human rights for example open up the world of culture, art, science, history, education, etc. They open up the options, show the merits of all options and hence can improve your volition. Constraining rules are also enabling rules. By limiting certain kinds of behavior they make other behavior possible, for example public discussion of objects of volition. Only in a public space protected by legal rights, where everybody is equal and where everybody can speak and listen in an equal way, can we examine our opinions and options and can we self develop.

The law is necessary because if there is no external control, then rights will be violated, security rights but also rights which protect the public space in which choices can appear. Some people will be victims of others and will not be free, not in any sense of the word. They cannot do as they like and they have no public life. And we can all be victims in certain circumstances. Laws and obedience are not just obstacles or impediments, limits on our freedom or elements of oppression. They are prerequisites for public life and therefore prerequisites for freedom as well because freedom needs public life.

Laws do not only limit the actions of people; they also link the actions of people because they create a public life. And these links make freedom possible. Laws are rules for public life and should not disappear. The state is a mechanism to coerce people, but this is not necessarily negative. On the contrary, coercion creates possibilities. The state creates, by way of coercion, the prerequisites for public life — such as security and human rights — and therefore creates the possibility of freedom.

A third problem with the limited freedom to do as one wishes is that this concept disregards a longstanding tradition which views freedom as autonomy. Individual autonomy, or the sense of having some measure of control over one's own life, is something different from the limited or unlimited individual freedom to do as you like. It is a more communal and less individualistic notion since it requires political self government through democratic participation.

Like freedom in the sense of self development, and unlike freedom as the (limited) ability to do as one wishes, autonomy is not separated from the state, is not a freedom outside of the state. It is necessarily a part of it and cannot survive without it. People usually engage in self government within state institutions, local or national. By determining the laws and rules which govern their lives, they govern themselves. In a democracy, the coercion of the law is the coercion of people over themselves. If people make their own laws, then obeying the law means obeying yourself and having control over your life.

In this respect, autonomy can be said to resemble freedom as the ability to do as you like, because people who obey themselves do as they like.

They decide for themselves and they are autonomous. They do not obey an external force and they are free from external rules and external coercion. All this is also demanded by the Hobbesian definition. The difference with the Hobbesian definition is that autonomy does not result from the isolated exercise of an individual will outside of state control. In autonomy, the ability to do as you like is mediated through political participation and legislation. And this is comparable to the way in which this ability is mediated through public life in the notion of freedom as self development (you can only do as you like when you know about the options and when the options appear in public).

Central to autonomy is the law. The law is an extension and expression of the people and of their convictions. Obeying a law is then merely a matter of internal coherence, of being in agreement with your own convictions and internal laws regarding the actions that can or cannot be done. People obey the law because they can recognize their convictions in the law and they can recognize their convictions because they make the law themselves. In a democracy, the people find the laws in themselves and agree with the laws which they obey. A law that forbids me to do what my conviction also forbids me to do, does not limit my freedom.

But the law in a democracy is not merely a simple expression of the will and the internal law of the people. People do not just recognize their prior convictions in the laws. The law or better the common act of legislation helps to form these convictions. Political participation shapes the will of the people. It is a more educated will than the will of an isolated individual because the political deliberations which precede the act of legislation have an educational effect. People get informed about alternatives, pros and cons, etc. So autonomy is similar to freedom as the ability to do as you want, but in a sense it is a better version of it because the quality of human volition is improved by it, just as it is improved by publicity. Freedom as self development improves volition by offering a public space in which to examine the objects of our will and to widen the options. Freedom as autonomy improves volition by allowing people to act together and establish laws.

If we temporarily put aside the problem of the democratic minority, then we see that autonomy is a very equal kind of freedom. There is an equal right to political participation, an equal identification with the law, the equal examination of options and pros and cons, etc.

Is self control an individual ability or one which is exercised together with others? It is clear I think that a community which governs itself gives more self control to its members than individuals who try to achieve this self control independently. Cooperation makes it easier to solve certain problems. If self control means determining your own life, then it also means being able to decide something and to solve problems. Autonomy is therefore best served by democratic political participation and cooperation.

If we look at freedom in this way, we can say that a tyrant is not more free than his subjects. Perhaps he is more free because he has a greater ability to do as he likes. But a tyrant does not have access to a political and public space which is indispensable for freedom in the sense of autonomy or self development. Such a space needs the protection of democracy and human rights and the equal participation of all, and is therefore incompatible with tyranny.

> The point of Herodotus' equation of freedom with no-rule was that the ruler himself was not free; by assuming the rule over others, he had deprived himself of those peers in whose company he could have been free. In other words, he had destroyed the political space itself, with the result that there was no freedom extant any longer, either for himself or for those over whom he ruled.[5]

The problem can also be framed in terms of the good life. Is our good life something individual and outside of politics and the public space, or is it something more communal? Does it mean that our private space has to be protected against others or does it also need others, their points of view, their criticism and their cooperation in shaping our lives? I think the latter is the case because without the public space in which others can appear and without the political space in which we can cooperate with others, our volition is of inferior quality. We may be able to do what we want, but what we want is not what would be best for us.

But what about the democratic minorities? Do they have equal freedom, equal autonomy? Of course, in a democracy there is always a minimum of external control. Only the majority exercises voluntary self legislation, self control and self obedience because only the majority accepts and desires the law voluntarily. The minority or even individuals belonging to the majority

---

5 Arendt 1990, op. cit., p. 31.

can decide to disagree with the law, because they do not identify with it or because they have a moment of weakness which disables the internal law.

The minorities' disagreement with the law does not necessarily force them to break the law; they can decide to respect the law because they do not wish to be punished, because they like order and predictability, or because they have an attitude of respect towards the law in general. But even if they do not break the law, this law is forced upon them by themselves. They don't have self control or autonomy. There is indirect external control and coercion, and hence not even freedom in Hobbes' definition. They don't obey themselves and cannot do as they like. The law does not come from the inside. It is not a part of the people in question even if they respect or accept it voluntarily for the reasons given above.

However, we can point to the fact that in a well functioning democracy everyone is now and again in the minority, which means that there is more or less equal autonomy across the population and over a longer period of time, and hence equal freedom. And secondly, although the minorities do not accept all majority laws, they are likely to accept the fundamental laws such as human rights which open the public space for majority and minority alike, and which therefore offer the minority freedom as self development, even while taking away, temporarily, freedom as autonomy.

The laws which exist and which I, as a member of the minority do not accept, limit my freedom in a certain sense. They limit the things I can do and the ways in which I can act, they limit my self control, but they do it in such a way that a public space comes into existence in which my freedom can unfold, freedom as self development.[6]

FREEDOM AND THE STATE

Freedom in every sense of the word — including the freedom to do as you like, at least if we want this to be an equal kind of freedom — needs the state and the rule of law. So entering into a state — metaphorically of course — is not the limitation of freedom but the start of it. For the proponents of the limited version of Hobbes' negative freedom, the state cannot create freedom. It only equalizes it by taking away some of it. The state always limits freedom because it is no more than a mechanism for coercion and security

---

6 Arendt 1994, op. cit., p. 81.

and hence takes away some of our power to do as we like, justifiably but also regrettably.

This reasoning implies some sort of natural or pre-political freedom which exists before and outside of the state, and which is partly surrendered in exchange for security by the theoretical or historical entry into the state-system (the so-called "contract"). But this natural freedom is a highly contestable concept, and not only because it is very unlikely that man lived in a situation of natural and unlimited freedom in those prehistorical times in which states or laws did not exist. At best, this natural freedom was or is highly unequal and other kinds of freedom were entirely impossible because there was no self government and no public life, or at least no stable, equally accessible and predictable public life protected by the state and the law.[7]

It is equally unlikely that the disappearance of the state will result in more freedom. A war of all against all is much more likely. The "chickens" among us need protection and protection is best provided by an impartial third party in order to avoid the spiral of revenge caused by self defense. This third party is almost always, and perhaps inevitably, the state. But even the limitation (rather than the disappearance) of the state to what is strictly required by the provision of protection, security and peace, will not result in more freedom. Social security, political participation and the protection of the public space are also requirements of freedom. A limited state may not be able to provide these institutions and may therefore harm freedom. Freedom is created on the basis of and after the law. The entry into a state is the foundation and the beginning of freedom instead of the surrender of freedom.

> The state is the actuality of concrete freedom. . . . Society and state . . . are the only situations in which freedom can be realised.[8]

Only a state can create self government and a public space in which autonomy and self development can become possible. Freedom is situated in the state and in politics. Instead of a necessary evil — necessary because of human nature and evil because of the limitations on freedom — we can see the state as something positive and the creator of freedom.

---

7 If there is no natural freedom, there may be natural rights. Rights and freedoms are not necessarily the same thing, even though the word "liberties" is often used as a synonym for the word "rights".

8 Hegel in Harrison, op. cit., p. 114.

So paradoxically, freedom can only exist together with obedience because only a state with its rules and laws can make freedom possible, both a simplistic negative freedom that is limited and hence equalized for all, and a freedom that is more than the simple ability to do as you like. Obedience to rules opens up the public and political space in which people can develop and can take control over their lives. Freedom is, therefore, not incompatible with power and coercion.

The state not only restricts freedom, and its elimination or limitation will not give us freedom, not even at the basic level of the ability to do as we like, at least if we want this ability to be equally distributed. A state limited to the provision of security will not provide this equality. Economic intervention by the state is also necessary. An equal limited freedom, autonomy and self development may not be safe in the hands of anarchists, libertarians, free marketers or proponents of the minimal state. All these kinds of freedom require more than constant attacks on the state. They require active involvement of the state, either to equalize freedom or to create its preconditions and institutions. In particular social security, political rights and civil rights are tools for this involvement, but only the latter are acceptable for the proponents of the minimal state.

Freedom in every sense of the word needs all types of human rights, economic, civil and political. The minimal state ideology only accepts state interventions for security when physical security is threatened by the freedom of others or by state violations of freedom rights. The goal is to force the state to limit its own interference and to force it to limit the harmful use of freedom by other citizen. That the state should actively interfere to build a public space and a political system of self government, to equalize the access to this space and system, particularly economically, and to equalize the ability to do as you want beyond the equalization offered by security, is politically controversial. Economic rights and affirmative action do not always enjoy majority support. But if coercion is justified for the sake of security, then why not for social security and anti-discrimination?

> [W]hy is avoiding coercion a supreme end that dominates all other ends? What makes noncoercion superior to justice, equality, freedom, security, happiness, and other values? If any of these ends are superior to noncoercion, then would not coercion be justified if it were the sole means in some situations for achieving the superior value? Alternatively, if one believes that the world of values is not dominated by a single absolute end but

is . . . a pluralistic universe, then one must make judgments about trade-offs between coercion and other values.[9]

From the libertarian point of view, the state cannot promote freedom. It always harms freedom because it is no more than a mechanism of coercion necessary to oppress evil originating from the state or from the free actions of our fellow-citizens, and coercion always takes away the power to do as you like. Libertarians accept that some freedom is taken away by the state, because they accept that freedom and security need to be balanced against each other and that freedom needs to be equalized and protected against the freedom of others. However, freedom is most important and state coercion for security and equality should therefore be kept to a minimum. Other values, such as autonomy, self government, self development and economic equality, which depend on state intervention and coercion, tend to get less attention in this worldview, even if they can be seen as prerequisites for freedom in a more profound sense of the word, in a sense which is different from the sum of the unhindered activities outside of the state and the law.

So the question is what kind and what degree of coercion we are ready to accept as a trade-off for our other values. If the freedom to do as you like is the only or the supreme value, then it seems that only coercion for security is acceptable. If you agree that not only insecurity and the freedom of others but also economic inequality can destroy the ability to do as you like, you may be willing to accept some kind of state coercion for the protection of economic security. And if you value autonomy, self government and self development, you may also accept state coercion for the creation of an equally accessible public and political space.

Freedom on the one hand and coercion, law, power, politics and the state on the other hand are not incompatible and one is not defined by the absence of the other. Freedom does not begin where politics, the state and coercion stop. Pushing back politics, the state and coercion can diminish freedom instead of increasing it. Freedom from politics may result in the end of freedom. Freedom is not the art of anti-politics. However, freedom and power are not just compatible. Freedom in the sense of autonomy is a kind of power, namely power over your own life.

Or course, it is obvious that not every kind of coercion by the state or the law is beneficial. A state which coerces in order to steal from the people or

---

9 Dahl, R.A. 1989, *Democracy and Its Critics*, New Haven/London: Yale University Press, p. 45-6.

oppress them, for example, can never promote freedom. Only a state that respects the longstanding principles of the rule of law, including human rights, can protect freedom because only such a state can promote security, self government, autonomy, public life, etc.

Freedom does not follow automatically from the coercion of the law. The law must be the right kind of law:

- It must protect human rights, in particular the security rights of possible victims but also the rights of the poor.

- It must protect the public space as a necessary condition for freedom in the sense of self development, and it can do so because it protects human rights.

- And it must be the product of the people if it is to promote autonomy.

The desire to keep state interference restricted is entirely justified. The number of limits on actions should indeed be as small as possible. The power of the state cannot be absolute or unlimited — we need a civil society, a free space beyond the reach of the limited state — but the minimum number of limits on actions is much larger than the number of limits necessary for security. Security is not the only value. Poverty as well can impair freedom, even at the basic level of the ability to do as you like. Hence, laws which eliminate poverty and redistribute wealth (as is demanded by economic rights) can also be acceptable limits on actions. Moreover, reducing the state to something very small and eliminating politics from society as much as we can, can harm political life and freedom in the sense of autonomy, at least as long as we continue to deny the distinction between politics and the state.

It is obvious that the extra-political sphere should not be considered as the only stronghold of freedom. Limiting politics, the state and coercion should not be our only worry. We should also try to make politics compatible with self government, autonomy and self development and we should try to see state coercion as something which is necessary for our freedom.

Coercion, if it is to promote equal freedom in different senses of the word, has to be:

1. Self coercion, when possible, because of autonomy and self control; and if not:

2. Limited coercion, limited in the sense it is:

- Compatible with human rights, especially the rights of the minority because the minority, while lacking autonomy, can use human rights for freedom in the sense of self development.
- Limited to what is necessary for equal freedom, security and public and political life.
- Legal coercion because otherwise it will not be limited. (A law is limited by definition. Coercion by persons is much more arbitrary and unlimited than coercion by the law because the meaning of personal commands is not as well-defined or as stable as the meaning of laws. Personal commands can be anything, whereas a law is what it is, it is written down, in a very specific manner, and it remains the same, otherwise there would be no reason to write it down. A tyrant also coerces, but he coerces in an unlimited way. In general, he does not use laws or if he does, he uses them in an improper way. The meaning of his laws is unlimited, unpredictable and changing. Moreover, his laws violate human rights and are aimed at particular groups in society and are not general or neutral as they are supposed to be).

3. Equal coercion (legal coercion is by definition equal coercion; the law rules over and coerces everybody in the same way).

Much of political philosophy is an attempt to answer the following question: how do we promote freedom without stumbling into anarchy, and how do we use power without stumbling into tyranny? If we believe that freedom gravitates towards anarchy, then we assume that freedom is no more than the ability to do as we like and that we should abolish all rules or as many rules as possible in order to protect freedom. And then we quickly discover the problem of anarchy, and not to mention the problem of the inequality which this kind of freedom produces. If insecurity, chaos and war are a threat to the freedom of some (to the freedom of the weak who can no longer do as they like), then they are also the ultimate expression of the freedom of others. Insecurity and anarchy are the consequences of our ability to do as we like and hence the consequence of our freedom.

However, if we redefine freedom as autonomy and self development, or even as the equal ability to do as you like, then we see that freedom needs rules and hence the danger of anarchy is averted. If power and coercion gravitate towards tyranny, then we assume that they are evil — maybe necessary but certainly evil — and that we should try to contain them as much as the development of human nature permits. However, if we accept that power and coercion not only constrain but also enable, that they create a public and political space which can be used for the development of freedom, then we start to see the state in a more positive light and we can put aside the fear of tyranny.

Who does not wish to be free and equal? I hope that this example of the way in which human rights (including political rights) can serve to protect important human values such as liberty and equality will convince the reader of the importance of human rights, and that the previous chapters will have given him or her some useful ideas to organize the practical realization of these rights.

REFERENCES

Akehurst, M. 1991, *A Modern Introduction to International Law*, London: Harper Collins

Arendt, H. 1979, *The Origins of Totalitarianism*, London: Harcourt/Brace

Arendt, H. 1990, *On Revolution*, Harmondsworth: Penguin Books

Arendt, H. 1994, *Tussen verleden en toekomst*, Leuven: Garant

Barber, B.R. 1984, *Strong Democracy, Participatory Politics for a New Age*, Berkeley/Los Angeles: University of California Press

Beetham, D. 1995, *Politics and Human Rights*, Oxford: Blackwell

Cassese, A. 1992, *International Law in a Divided World*, Oxford: Clarendon Press

Cliteur, P.B. 1997, *De filosofie van mensenrechten*, Nijmegen: Ars Aequi Libri

Dahl, R.A. 1989, *Democracy and Its Critics*, New Haven/London: Yale University Press

Donnelly, J. 1996, *Universal Human Rights in Theory and Practice*, London: Cornell University Press

Fukuyama, F. 1992, *The End of History and the Last Man*, Harmondsworth: Penguin Books

Harrison, R. 1996, *Democracy*, London/New York: Routledge

Hobbes, T. 1984, *Leviathan*, Harmondsworth: Penguin

Huntington, S. 1998, *The Clash of Civilizations and the Remaking of World Order*, Simon & Schuster

Kekes, J. 1999, *Against Liberalism*, London: Cornell University Press

Little, D. 1996, "Tolerance, Equal Freedom, and Peace", in United States Institute of Peace, available online at http://www.usip.org/religionpeace/rehr/equalfree. html

Mourgeon, J. 1996, *Les droits de l'homme*, Paris: PUF

Nelson, W.N. 1980, *On Justifying Democracy*, London: Routledge and Kegan

Rawls, J. 1999, *A Theory of Justice*, Oxford: Oxford University Press

Rials, S. 1982, *Textes constitutionnels français*, Paris: Presses Universitaires de France

Schmitt, C. 1993, *Verfassungslehre*, Berlin: Duncker & Humblot

Spagnoli F. 2003, *Homo Democraticus, On the Universal Desirability and the not so Universal Possibility of Democracy and Human Rights*, London: Cambridge Scholars Press

Spagnoli, F. 2004, *Democratic Imperialism*, London: Cambridge Scholars Press

Vienna Declaration and Programme of Action 1993, Adopted by the World Conference on Human Rights, doc UN A/CONF.157/23

Appendix: List of Human Rights

This is a list of the most important human rights included in the Universal Declaration of Human Rights (UDHR), the International Covenant on Civil and Political Rights (ICCPR), the International Covenant on Economic, Social and Cultural Rights (ICESCR) and the European Convention for the Protection of Human Rights and Fundamental Freedoms (ECPHR) (the complete texts are available in different locations on the Internet):

1. Civil Rights or Freedom Rights:
   - Equality of rights without discrimination
   - Life
   - Security and integrity of the person
   - Protection against slavery, torture and cruel or inhuman punishment (humane treatment when detained)
   - Protection against arbitrary arrest or detention (arrest or detention only on the basis of a law and with prompt notice of the charges)
   - A public, fair and prompt trial before an independent, impartial and competent judge
   - Presumption of innocence until proven guilty
   - Means necessary for your defense

- Protection against compulsory confession

- The right not to testify against yourself

- "Ne bis in idem", no two convictions or punishments for the same offence

- Case reviewed by a higher tribunal

- Protection against "ex post facto" laws, laws established after the deed

- "Nullum crimen sine lege", there is no offense without a law

- Recognition as a person before the law

- Equality before the law and equal protection by the law

- Judicial protection of rights and access to legal remedies for rights violations (the right to apply to a court which offers redress for violations)

- Protection of privacy, family, home and correspondence

- Freedom of movement and residence

- Asylum from persecution

- The right not to be deprived of your nationality, the right to change your nationality

- Protection against arbitrary expulsion of nationals and aliens

- Leave and return to your country

- The right to marry and beget a family of your choice

- Protection of the family

- The right to own property

- Freedom of thought and religion

- Freedom of expression (seeking, receiving and imparting information regardless of borders)

- The absence of attacks on your honor and reputation

- Freedom of assembly and association (including the right to leave an association)

2. Political Rights or Democratic Rights:

- Political participation, directly and through freely chosen representatives

- Equal access to public service, the right to be elected

- The will of the people is the basis of the authority of government
- Periodic and genuine elections
- Universal and equal suffrage
- Secret vote

3. Social, Economic and Cultural Rights:

- Social security
- A certain standard of living
- Work, of your own choice and under favorable conditions
- Protection for the unemployed, the elderly, the disabled and sick persons
- Fair wages and equal wages for equal work
- Free trade unions (right to form and join)
- Strike
- Rest and leisure
- Food, clothing and housing
- Health care
- Special protection for children and mothers
- Education
- Participation in the cultural life of the community
- Self-determination
- International solidarity

One might perhaps ask why I only mention the UDHR, the ICCPR, the ICESCR and the ECPHR. There are indeed dozens of other conventions and declarations concerning human rights. In some cases they deal with human rights in general; in other cases only with some specific rights or sets of rights. However, the fact is that these documents have become the international standard in matters of human rights.

INDEX